THEORIES OF TRUTH, MODELS OF USEFULNESS

TOWARD A REVOLUTION IN THE FIELD OF PSYCHOTHERAPY

Alvin R. Mahrer PhD

University of Ottawa, Canada

WHURR PUBLISHERS
LONDON AND PHILADELPHIA

© 2004 Whurr Publishers Ltd
First published 2004
by Whurr Publishers Ltd
19b Compton Terrace
London N1 2UN England and
325 Chestnut Street, Philadelphia PA 19106 USA

British Library Cataloguing in Publication Data

A catalogue record for this book
is available from the British Library.

ISBN 1 86156 411 2

Typeset by Adrian McLaughlin, a@microguides.net
Printed and bound in the UK by Athenæum Press Limited, Gateshead, Tyne & Wear

Contents

Preface

Is this book for you?

This is a preface with the honest mission of trying to give you enough of a glimpse to help you decide whether this book can reach you or invite you to listen and know what this book has to say.

Characteristics of an interested reader

As I was writing this book, especially the last few drafts, I pictured people who might be reading it. There were different people, with different characteristics. I hope that some of these characteristics come close to your own.

Some interest in the field of psychotherapy, although you are outside the profession

The key is that there is something about psychotherapy that is of interest to you. You may be a fan or a critic, or a little of both. You may have some acquaintance with the field or none at all. You may be having sessions with a professional psychotherapist, and so are many of your friends, or the very idea strikes you as somewhat alien. Psychotherapy may have little or nothing to do with your own work. Yet there is some interest in psychotherapy, whether it is a rather faint glow or a genuine interest.

What can make this book attractive to you is that you are genuinely outside the field of psychotherapy. You probably are also free of many of the foundational beliefs of those inside the field. You probably are free of their ingrained ways of thinking, their particular mind-sets, the notions and ideas that they almost take for granted. You are probably outside their culture. All of this can put you in a better position to see and appreciate what this book is trying to say and bring about.

You do not have to be sophisticated or even very knowledgeable about psychotherapy. A little interest is enough. You do not have to know the jargon or the technical vocabulary about psychotherapy. Much of it may be thought of as psychobabble anyhow, and I explain enough for you to know what is important for an appreciation of what this book is seeking to say. You do not have to be able to recite the prominent psychotherapies, or to know anything about psychotherapy research. Just a little bit of interest is sufficient.

Whether inside or outside the field of psychotherapy, you have some interest in the 'ideas' part of the field

This book talks about the 'idea' of 'theories of truth' and the 'idea' of 'models of usefulness'. The emphasis is more on the ideas and less on the applied parts of the field. If ideas have some appeal to you, this book can be for you.

Although the emphasis is on ideas, the implications are exceedingly practical and applied. If the field shifts, even a little bit, from thinking almost exclusively in terms of theories of truth to being able to think in terms of models of usefulness, there can be almost revolutionary implications down at the practical level of applied work. You may be a practical or applied person. This book will probably appeal to you if you are also an 'ideas' person.

Whether inside or outside the field, you are open to the possibility of a revolutionary shift in psychotherapy

If you have even a slight openness to a revolutionary shift, this book is for you, and you are the reader sought by this book. If enough people in the field can actually shift from theories of truth to models of usefulness, this field can undergo a revolutionary shift forward. Are you open, even a little bit, to allowing for the possibility of a wholesale revolution in the field of psychotherapy? If so, you are probably an interested reader.

Could you be interested in what this book has to say?

My job here is to give you the essence of what this book has to say, an honest and accurate glimpse or preview, to help you decide whether you are interested in reading this book.

Theories of truth: what they are and how they virtually dominate the field

Theories of truth are made up of things that are presumed to be true, and they do their best to get at the truth of the things that they study. There are lots of different theories of truth, and they do not all believe in the truth of the same things. But, collectively, theories of truth believe in the truth of such things as schizophrenia, egos, basic emotions, cognitions and cognitive structures, basic needs and drives, psychopathology, growth forces, stages of psychological development, addictive personalities, mental illnesses and disorders, and hundreds of other things that are thought of as true.

Accordingly, there are theories of schizophrenia, theories of personality, theories of anxiety, theories of psychopathology, theories of child development. Theories of truth try to get at the true nature of these things, at the basic structure and content of things such as schizophrenia or cognitions, basic needs or stages of psychological development.

Theories of truth try to get at the kinds or types or categories of things that are true.

- What are the categories of basic needs?
- What are the kinds of schizophrenia?
- What are the official types of mental illnesses and disorders?
- What are the true causes of these true things?
- How does a person who ends up with a severe depressive psychopathology develop?
- What are the determinants over the person's life?
- What determinants were inherited?
- What causes lie somewhere in the brain?

A theory of truth gets at the true kinds, types and causes of these true things.

Research is carried out to confirm or disconfirm the truth of what theories of truth believe is true. It is to establish the truth of principles and dictums and laws, such as the law of effect. It is to get at the truth, to contribute to the body of truth, to enable theories to approximate more closely the truth of what the theories hold as true.

Models of usefulness: how they differ greatly from theories of truth and are exceedingly rare in psychotherapy

One way that models of usefulness are different from theories of truth is that the field of therapy is filled with theories of truth, and models of usefulness are virtually nowhere to be found. But this doesn't explain what 'models of usefulness' are.

There are two main characteristics of models of usefulness, two ways that identify them as exceedingly different from theories of truth:

1. In theories of truth, the emphasis, or premium, is on getting at the truth of the things that they study, their subject matter. In models of useful- ness, the emphasis – the premium – is on the use, getting the job done, bringing about some particular change. The model is a tool that is designed and useful for some designated use.

    Start with some designated use such as unlocking that locked door, getting to that distant planet, becoming the person one is capable of becoming, growing larger tomatoes, stopping the roof from leaking, becoming free of that awful feeling of dread when you are inside the ele- vator at the top of the extremely tall building. These are the designated aims, goals, things that you want to accomplish. Models are conceptual tools that can help you achieve what you want to achieve, get what you want to get. In models of usefulness, the premium is usefulness. The worth or the test of a model is its ability to be useful.

2. Theories of truth accept the truth of their component parts, the things that they study, their subject matter. Models of usefulness start with their intended uses, the real changes they are to help bring about. Then models of usefulness are constructed out of parts that are 'convenient fictions'. Models of usefulness invent things, fabricate things, make things up. These things are unreal, invented fictions, fictions that are convenient, useful.

    Models of usefulness invent things, create models, build pictorialized metaphors, because they are useful in getting the job done, in achieving the goal. The use is probably real and true. You can tell if the door unlocks or the roof no longer leaks. But the conceptual model you create to make sense of and help achieve your use is made up of things that are unreal, fictitious, but so convenient, so useful.

    Models of usefulness can invent things such as schizophrenia, psychic energy, core cognitive structures, stress tolerance motivations, deeper potentials for experiencing and hundreds of other things. Models of use-fulness can invent elves and goblins, devils and gods, seasonal affective disorders and depressive disorders. They are not thought of as real and true. They are thought of as convenient fictions, useful in helping to achieve the use for which the model of usefulness was created to help achieve.

Interest in the revolution following movement of the field of psychotherapy from theories of truth to models of usefulness

This book invites the field of psychotherapy to leave a little room for models of usefulness. But this invitation comes with a warning. If the field moves toward welcoming models of usefulness, the field is there-by moving toward a wholesale revolution. Are you interested in taking a closer look at this revolution?

Here is a small sample package of what the field of psychotherapy would probably give up, discard, when the revolution comes:

- The field would let go of its hundreds of tests, scales and inventories that are supposed to measure the things that theories of truth believe are real and true. A model of usefulness can invent something called 'deeper potentials for experiencing', but this is acknowledged as unreal, and therefore models of usefulness would decline trying to build tests and scales and inventories to measure a deeper potential for experiencing color or weight, length or width, speed or hardness, density or volume. The revolution would probably see the end of the era of measuring all sorts of things that are not real or true, from schizophrenia to basic needs, from affect tolerance to depressive residuals, from seasonal affec-tive disorders to the hundreds of other things that theories of truth believe are real and true.

- It would let go of trying to locate where the 'convenient fictions' are in the body. There would be virtually no efforts to see whether deeper potentials for experiencing are located in the frontal lobe or the pituitary, in the bloodstream or the armpit. The field would relegate the work of seeing where schizophrenia is located in the body to those who believe in theo-ries of truth.

- It would let go of trying to get at the structure, the content, the way these convenient fictions are organized, made up. You can take apart an eyeball and learn more about its structure. You can do the same with other things that you think of as real and true. You can study the structure and the content of things such as a volcano, a root of a tree, a drop of water, a clock. On the other hand, if you thought of these things as convenient fictions, you would probably not try to uncover the structure and content of schizophrenia, a core cognitive structure, psychic energy or an ego. They are not real and true. In this way of thinking, they have no real and true structure and content.

- It would let go of trying to arrive at the true number and kinds and types of things that it invents, its convenient fictions. How many kinds and types of deeper potentials for experiencing are there? The answer depends on how many are useful to invent, rather than on how many there really and truly are. In the same way, the field would be able to give up looking for how many kinds and types of invented things such as basic emotions, basic drives, mental illnesses, stages of development, self-defeating cognitions there are, and the hundreds of other things that are invented or made up.

- It would let go of trying to get at the causes of things that are merely convenient fictions. If there is an explosion in the warehouse, if the roof leaks or if an airplane crashes, it can make sense to look for causes, especially if these things are considered to be real and true. On the other hand, it makes little sense to look for the real and true causes of things that are merely convenient fictions. What accounts for this person having a depressed personality, developing schizophrenia, having low psychic energy, having a weak ego? Do the causes lie in the birth experience, the family support system, the order in which siblings were born, the learning experiences during childhood? There would be an abandoning of a search for the real and true causes of things that are unreal and untrue, invented, made up, fictitious.

- It would let go of doing research that is mainly aimed at confirming the truth of what the field believes is true. Do males and females have different deeper potentials for experiencing? If you believe that is true, you can do research to confirm or disconfirm it. If, however, deeper potentials for experiencing are invented convenient fictions, it makes considerably less sense to check out the truth of your belief that males and females do indeed have different deeper potentials for experiencing. A great many of the reasons for doing research would be let go if the beliefs that are to be confirmed or disconfirmed are accepted as merely convenient fictions in the first place.

This is just a small package of implications, of what would probably happen if the field granted some room for models of usefulness. These implications could well be revolutionary. This book seeks to tell us about many more implications there are to the field accepting models of usefulness, rather than being almost exclusively composed of theories of truth.

Is there even a glow of interest in the revolutionary changes that might well occur if the field of psychotherapy provided some room for models of usefulness, or actually shifted from theories of truth to models of usefulness? If the answer is yes, this book is for you and you are the reader that this book is looking for.

How did this book come about?

I hope that giving you a picture of how this book came about can help in your decision of whether or not to read it.

The innocent beginnings

I dabbled in philosophy of science during my doctoral years, from the late 1940s to the early 1950s. There were a small number of doctoral students who read a little philosophy of science as a kind of underground – pornographic – reading, quite aside from the material of our courses.

I continued reading philosophy of science when I began practising, training, doing research, teaching. However, these readings were rather more like a sporadic avocation than a serious or formal pursuit. They seemed interesting, although I rarely if ever connected that material with what I was doing in my professional work. I could have, I might have, perhaps someone else would have, but I did not see how my armchair reading of the philosophy of science had any real connection to what I was doing in my professional work. It did. I just did not see any connections.

The serious beginnings

Things changed when I began having doubts and uncertainties about my work, what I was doing, and especially when I began to try to figure out my own position on many basic issues, and my own answers to basic questions. I was looking for what I seemed to think. I was looking for clarity. I was not especially trying to come up with my own positions or answers.

I was face to face with some basic questions, some basic issues:

- What were the origins of how and why a person became whatever sort of person he or she became?
- How is one theory of personality better than another?
- Why is it that people with different theories seem to have so much trouble talking seriously with one another?
- Was there really something called schizophrenia?
- What accounts for the comings and goings of painful and unhappy feelings?
- What are the limits of how deeply and how broadly a person is able to change?
- What can a person become?
- How can dreams be accounted for?
- How can you tell if something is real and true, especially if some people believe that it is real and true and others do not?
- Is there really a mind and a body, and do they affect one another?
- How does a person undergo substantial change in who and what the person is?

In my sophomore attempts to answer these questions for myself, I slowly realized that I was coming face to face with ways of thinking, with issues and questions, that were the subject matter of the philosophy of science. The other side of this realization was that the field of psychotherapy did not offer much help when trying to answer these questions, and finding my own position on these issues. To get reasonably clear about the serious matters that faced me in the field of psychotherapy, I probably needed to understand more about what the philosophy of science had to say. Here were the serious beginnings of my trying to learn from the philosophy of science.

Are these some implications for psychotherapy?

Philosophers of science did not talk much about the field of psychotherapy. As I turned seriously to the philosophy of science, I began to see implications for psychotherapy. I began to see powerful implications for psychotherapy. Indeed, the implications seemed revolutionary. If I am even close in understanding the implications, they would seem to turn the field of psychotherapy inside out, to put it on a radically different foundation, to revolutionize psychotherapy. This was exciting, powerful. It was also unnerving, scary.

Of the many things that I believe philosophers of science offered, one had to do with a distinction between what they seemed to refer to as theories and models, theories of truth and models of usefulness. I believed that I could grasp this distinction, and I was fascinated, excited and scared about what seemed to be the powerful, revolutionary implications if the field of psychotherapy accepted, and perhaps even adopted, this distinction.

So I asked these philosophers of science. I mentioned articles in journals or chapters in books, and asked if I got the main points that were there in this literature from the philosophy of science. They said, in general: 'Yes, you got the main points, kind of.'

I pointed to particular articles and chapters. These seem to distinguish between theories of truth and models of usefulness, and show the advantages that each seems to have, especially in fields such as physics, mathematics and other related fields. Am I even close here? The philosophers of science said, in general: 'Yes, you seem to understand, kind of.'

Then I went on to what was most exciting and scary for me. If there can be a distinction between 'theories of truth' and 'models of usefulness', it seems to me that here are some powerful, revolutionary implications for the field of psychotherapy. Am I even close here? The philosophers of science said, in general: 'We cannot say with much confidence because most of us have little or no serious knowledge of the field of psychotherapy. In other words, we don't know.'

This was bothersome. So I turned to some of my colleagues in psychotherapy, some mainly in psychotherapy practice, some mainly in psychotherapy theory and some mainly in psychotherapy research.

I wanted to know if they also saw a difference between what might be called 'theories of truth' and 'models of usefulness'. If they did, did they also see these implications for psychotherapy? If they did, did they also see these implications as powerful, as revolutionary, for the field of psychotherapy theory, research and practice?

I asked my colleagues in correspondence, in reading their writings and writings that they recommended. I talked face to face with some colleagues, sometimes just the two of us, sometimes in small groups. I organized symposia on this general topic. I guest-edited special sections or theme issues of journals on this general topic. There were three general reactions from these colleagues:

1. Most were simply not interested. They were not especially interested in what may be seen as a distinction between theories of truth and models of usefulness, or in implications for the field of psychotherapy.

2. Many of my colleagues pointed out how wrong I was. They already were well acquainted with such a distinction. There are no solid grounds for such a distinction. The field of psychotherapy already accommodates both theories of truth and models of usefulness. Naming such implications was erroneous thinking. They were much better acquainted with the philosophy of science, and I was wrong in seeing both such a distinction and such implications. I was making far too much of such a distinction, and the implications I saw were examples of my wrong-headedness.

   These kinds of reactions were both encouraging and discouraging. I tried to use these reactions to become somewhat clearer in identifying theories of truth and models of usefulness, and especially in seeing their implications for psychotherapy, whether these implications were minor or major, cosmetic or perhaps quite revolutionary.

3. Some colleagues were also thinking the way I was thinking. They saw what I saw. For these colleagues, their way of thinking already distinguished between theories of truth and models of usefulness. They shared some of my surprise and excitement in seeing more and more of the implications for psychotherapy. They helped me see even more of the revolutionary implications.

Do you see what I believe I see?

If I can switch from theories of truth to models of usefulness, I believe that there can be some powerful, comprehensive, exciting, revolutionary shifts forward in psychotherapy. Philosophers of science see these powerful implications in the sciences that they are inclined to study as their favorite subject matter. Most people in psychotherapy are either uninterested in or apparently antagonistic to seeing these revolutionary implications. Thankfully, some people in psychotherapy are inclined to see what I believe I see.

This volume gradually emerged because: (1) virtually the entire field of psychotherapy thinks in terms of theories of truth, (2) if the field can allow some room for models of usefulness, I do believe that it is heading toward a revolutionary shift forward and (3) I have a kind of naïve hope that sufficient numbers of people, both in and near the field of psychotherapy, can be ready to consider 'models of usefulness'.

If you decide this book is for you

I hope that you have some of the characteristics of an interested reader. I hope that you have at least a spark of interest in what this book has to say to you. I hope that this prefatory glimpse has been sufficient to help you decide whether or not this book is for you.

I also hope that you are willing to let me know what you think. Please write to me at Alvin R. Mahrer PhD, School of Psychology, University of Ottawa, Ottawa, Canada K1N 6N5. My email address is amahrer@uottawa.ca.

Alvin R. Mahrer

Chapter 1

Introduction

In this work there is a larger, more general aim and a smaller, more specific one.

To revolutionize the foundations of psychotherapy: the larger aim

The larger, longer-range, grandiose aim is to provide a qualitatively new foundation for the field of psychotherapy. Or at least the aim is to head in this direction.

One way to begin is to work with the present foundations, the anchoring structure of the field, the basic cornerstones, the fundamental principles, and gradually to develop them, carry them forward, to modify and improve the foundations of the field. This way relies on gradual advances in theory and research and a faith in the gradual advancement of the field, including its foundational structure. I am not following this path.

Another way to advance the field, the way that I prefer, is to open up the possibility of relocating the field on a whole new foundation, to try and encourage a wholesale paradigm shift. This way includes proposing a radical change in mind-set, in the actual foundations of the whole field of psychotherapy theory, research and practice. This way includes direct frontal attacks on the basic pillars of psychotherapy, gross violations of what is generally taken for granted, and a genuine constructive revolution toward a radically different foundation.

However, this is the longer-range aim. It is the spirit fuelling the smaller, more explicit aim.

To allow some room for models of usefulness in psychotherapy: the smaller aim

A baby step toward a wholesale revolution is for psychotherapy to at least know about, appreciate and be reasonably familiar with, and it is hoped allow a little room for, models of usefulness. I intend to make the following case:

1. I believe that most psychotherapists think in terms of theories of truth, whether they say so or not. Theories of truth are one basic pillar in psychotherapy. Thinking in terms of theories of truth is so exceedingly common that it is virtually ingrained, entrenched, almost without any plausible alternative. I will try to spell out precisely what I mean by 'theories of truth'.

2. There is such a thing as models of usefulness. Although these are relatively well known and appreciated in many other fields, they are virtual strangers to the general field of psychotherapy theory, research and practice. I will try to provide an introduction to 'models of usefulness', to explain what is meant by that phrase.

3. There are some basic and fundamental differences between theories of truth and models of usefulness. I will try to spell out some major differences.

4. I believe that there are some preferential features and advantages of models of usefulness over theories of truth. Furthermore, these preferential features and advantages can have extensive and powerful implications across psychotherapy, from its theory to its research, from its practice to its education and training. I will try to sketch out these preferential features and advantages, and also the revolutionary possibilities for the field.

5. Virtually the entire field of psychotherapy seems to have a collective mind-set of theories of truth. My intention is for some psychotherapists to let go of the virtually universal theories of truth and to go ahead and actually adopt a 'models-of-usefulness' mind-set or, perhaps more realistically, for some psychotherapists to allow some tolerable room for models of usefulness. I will try to make a case on behalf of this intent.

6. If this could come about, it would be a significant step toward a revolution in psychotherapy.

I know that these aims are grandiose and revolutionary. A great deal depends on the reader.

Openness to the possibility of a revolution in psychotherapy

I am hoping for even a few psychotherapists who are at least a little bit open to the possibility of a revolution, either a revolution in general or a revolutionary possibility of thinking in terms of models of usefulness. These few psychotherapists might be mainly theorists, researchers, practitioners, teachers or administrators. Even a few would do.

A great deal depends on the mind-set, on your built-in, intrinsic outlook or way of thinking. I am looking for psychotherapists with a receptive mind-set.

A mind-set with some room for the possibility of a revolution?

I hope that you are one of the rare psychotherapists whose mind-set allows some genuine dialogue, some room for openness to something other than what is taken for granted in your own way of thinking. You are able to give a fair hearing to knowing what is meant by models of usefulness even though you don't think in those terms. In your mind-set, it can be possible, if a fair enough case can be made, that you will allow some room for models of usefulness, even though the room is small and off to the side.

I am hoping that your mind-set can allow some room for the possibility of a revolution. That is enough. I am not trying to convince you to become part of the revolution, not even to embrace models of usefulness. It is enough that you can have a glow of welcoming receptivity.

A mind-set with little or no room for the possibility of a revolution?

If you are like many other psychotherapists, your mind-set has essentially no room for the possibility of a revolution. You think in terms of theories of truth, and that very mind-set is essentially closed tight against even granting a fair hearing to the mere idea of models of usefulness.

In a sense, the common mind-set of theories of truth is caught in a bind. It holds that the scientific pursuit of truth values openness to new ideas, to new ways of thinking, even to new cosmologies. However, there is a serious and guarded limit, and that limit is a new idea whose revolutionary possibilities include the threat to the mind-set of theories of truth! Such a revolution is forbidden. It may be safely talked about on paper, in abstract scientific discourse perhaps, in principle, but not when there is a very real threat to the very mind-set of theories of truth. That is going too far.

To this mind-set, merely discussing models of usefulness is anathema. It is seen as an attack on theories of truth, a parade of complaints, a deliberate looking for flaws and weaknesses in the ordinary mind-set of theories of truth. Psychotherapists with this mind-set will probably be inclined to resist the idea of models of usefulness, to find fault with this alternative, to counterattack, to fight. They will be inclined to reject the revolutionary possibility, to make sure that it is not published, to set it aside, to marginalize it, trivialize it, ignore it. They will be protected against sufficient proof by calling upon the dilemma of the inevitably insufficient case.

Show me the proof: the dilemma of the inevitably insufficient case

Psychotherapists with the mind-set of theories of truth are almost forced by their own mind-set to consider themselves open to evidence. When the evidence is sufficient, this mind-set is supposed to alter its notions and ideas, even what it has been taking for granted as true. This mind-set values itself as evidence-based. Provide sufficient proof, and the mind-set is supposed to weigh the evidence objectively and fairly. You are trying to present a case for models of usefulness? Go ahead.

However, and here is where the dilemma begins to emerge, this mind-set typically sets itself to be convinced by increasingly greater mounds of data, proof, logical arguments, convincing evidence. Keep trying to construct a convincing case. Cite studies. Cite more studies. Keep trying to construct a convincing case. For virtually every point, just try to assemble a convincing case that is solidly convincing, backed by an impressive phalanx of authorities, incontrovertible evidence and proof. Try to construct a case that is powerfully solid, academically sound, scientifically impressive. Keep trying. We will decide and let you know when your case is sufficient.

The dilemma takes center stage when it becomes refreshingly and whimsically clear that no such case can be constructed. No matter how strong the case, it is never going to be sufficient to defeat the theories-of-truth mind-set. What could possibly constitute the reasonable evidence that would be sufficient for this mind-set to give itself up, to see the virtues of models of usefulness, to abandon the theories-of-truth mind-set in favor of the rival mind-set, or even to allow for the possibility of a little room for models of usefulness? What is the likelihood that a case could ever be sufficient? Or is the very attempt defeated at the outset? It is at this point that the dilemma is exceedingly present and alive. No such case can ever be sufficient. This is the dilemma of the inevitably insufficient case. Given the mind-set of theories of truth, the attempt is virtually fruitless from the very beginning.

I sincerely hope that you have a mind-set that can allow for even the slender possibility of a revolution and one that can be open to the possibility of a little room for 'models of usefulness'.

Talking especially to the practitioner: the revolution

Yes, this revolution is talking to the psychotherapy theorist and researcher and teacher. They are invited to think about theories of truth and models of usefulness, and to pay some attention to the latter, at least in providing some room for them.

It can be easy for the practitioner to take a position that this stuff has little or nothing to do with actual practice, that it deals with conceptual matters that theorists and researchers usually try to convince practitioners are 'relevant', and can make a difference to practitioners.

I am cheerfully going to throw myself into that trap, i.e. I do believe that 'theories of truth' and 'models of usefulness' are conceptual matters. But, and this is a massive 'but', I am also convinced that the implications of letting go of our theories of truth and adopting models of usefulness are so vast, so deep, so sweeping, that in a single stroke the field will have stepped into a whole other world, and will have undergone a radical revolution.

I am convinced that most practitioners have deeply ingrained, broad, fundamental ways in which they think, that these ways of thinking have profound effects on what practitioners actually do in their practice, and that these ways of thinking and acting are done essentially without keen awareness of them. I am convinced that if these practitioners allow themselves to see what theories of truth are, and what models of usefulness are, then they are bringing themselves to the edge of profound changes in their actual practice.

Here is my challenge to the practitioner: Chapter 2 tries to clarify what distinguishes 'models of usefulness' from the almost universal 'theories of truth'. Do your best to appreciate the difference, to be able to see what is there before you as 'models of usefulness'. Chapter 3 spells out some preferential features of models of usefulness over theories of truth. This chapter provides the main section in which you can see for yourself what adopting a model of usefulness can do to your practice, how a model can make for magnificent, in-depth, sweeping, powerful, revolutionary changes in virtually every aspect of your practice.

Here is the direct challenge: I dare you to be able to spell out the case for adopting a model of usefulness. You don't have to adopt the model mind-set. You can decline, refuse, remain absolutely unchanged. Just be able to put into words the case for each way that adopting a model of usefulness is presented as making a significant difference in your practice. I am talking about practice, not about theory or research, but down-to-earth, practical, applied practice.

If you can meet the challenge, you win, and I will give you my precious bicycle. If you fail, then you lose, and the devil will make sure that you will henceforth have a mind-set of models of usefulness, for ever.

The revolution talks to theorists and researchers and teachers, but it is talking especially to practitioners. Almost every page is whispering to the practitioner that the applications and implications are widespread, powerful and exceedingly revolutionary.

Promoting the idea of models of usefulness, rather than any particular models

This book will have succeeded if the field of psychotherapy, or even a fair number of psychotherapists, take what I believe is a revolutionary step of at least looking favorably on the idea of models of usefulness, of welcoming the idea, of allowing some room for the development of models of usefulness. I have in mind psychotherapists who are primarily practitioners, theorists, researchers, teacher–trainers or students, or people who will someday fill those roles.

This seems to qualify as a revolutionary step, especially if you are inclined to agree that the field is virtually wall-to-wall theories of truth, with few if any models of usefulness.

As you consider what this volume has to say, you may well be inclined to wonder what particular model of usefulness I am espousing, and especially if I am trying to promote my own experiential model of psychology (Mahrer, 1989), psychotherapy (Mahrer, 1996/2004) or self-transformation (Mahrer, 2002b). There are at least two reasons why I am not trying to promote my experiential model:

1. I believe that the revolutionary step is for the field to welcome the idea of 'models of usefulness', and that is far more important than trying to promote any particular model, even my own.

2. Wonderful as my experiential model is, there are pitifully few alternative models. I believe it is far more important that the field first welcome the idea of models of usefulness, and then proceed to develop some worthwhile models, only later having the luxury of deciding which of an exciting number of models are best for given uses, aims and goals. The bottom line is that I am not trying to promote my own experiential model of usefulness.

Two apologies and two pleas to the reader

When it comes to the philosophy of science, I am about at the level of a sophomore student who appreciates what that field can have to say to psychotherapy. As I borrowed so much from philosophers of science, it was reassuring for some people to say that I was reasonably accurate and fair in what I borrowed and in what sense I made of the writings in the field of the philosophy of science.

On the other hand, most of the readers are likely to be psychotherapists, probably practitioners but also psychotherapists who may be involved in teaching, research, theory, administration. To you, I make two apologies and two pleas.

Dull and non-clinical, rather than inspiring and revolutionary, content

If I wanted to hoist a placard and parade around the field of psychotherapy, the placard might say: (1) there are theories of truth and models of usefulness and (2) adopt a model and become a revolutionary.

If a few psychotherapists were gracious enough to ask me to tell them more about it, my impression is that most of them would soon either politely walk away or fall asleep. For one thing, most of the content is not particularly familiar territory. It deals more with the philosophy of science, theories of truth and models of usefulness. It does not deal mainly with the more familiar topics under psychotherapy theory, research or clinical practice. The reader is asked to consider material that is not the usual material for most readers of psychotherapy literature. As you read, you are entitled to wonder what this has to do with psychotherapy, with psychotherapy theory, research or education/training, or especially with psychotherapy practice. I apologize in advance for much of the content that you will be reading. I will walk with you in what is likely to be some unfamiliar territory.

For another thing, not only is much of the content relatively unfamiliar territory, but also what you will be reading is probably going to seem not very inspirational or revolutionary. As I will be trying to build a case on behalf of models, much of what you will read will consist of case building, of arguments, and you are entitled to regard paragraph after paragraph as rather dense, dull, plodding, perhaps wandering around without going directly to the featured bottom line.

This is one thing for which I apologize. There is another.

The disquieting, uneasy, disturbing nature of gradually revealed revolutionary implications

Even though the content may be somewhat unfamiliar and the case building somewhat monotonous, the case is to invite the field into a wholesale revolution. Sometimes the revolutionary implications are spelled out directly. Sometimes the reader can sense the direction in which the case is headed. Each topic, each page – indeed, most paragraphs – can sketch out, preview or reveal the revolutionary implications.

For some readers, the gradually revealed revolutionary implications can be exciting. However, for many readers what they will gradually see can be unfriendly, disquieting, uneasy, disturbing. You may well be inclined to turn away, to sense what is coming and to find fault, criticize, attack, pick at, object, raise counterarguments, dislike what you are reading. After all, most revolutions are not especially welcomed by those whom the revolution displaces.

I offer these two apologies in advance to the reader. I also sincerely implore the reader to accept two pleas.

The intended payoff as revolution in psychotherapy

The unabashed intention is to help move the field in the direction of a wholesale revolution where at least some psychotherapy theorists, researchers, teacher–trainers, administrators and especially practitioners adopt models of usefulness. As will be shown, this can well mean a revolutionary shift for the field as a whole, including revolutionary changes in theorizing, in what research is for and how to go about doing research, in education/training, and also in so many aspects of practice. My plea is that you keep this in mind as you read.

Entertain serious consideration of allowing some room for models of usefulness

This is the more practical, more realistic invitation to the reader. Even if you do not adopt models of usefulness, my plea is that you accept enough about models to grant them a little room in the field. That is enough.

The aim of Chapter 2 is to present a case for drawing a friendly distinction between theories of truth and models of usefulness. The distinction is friendly because it is more a matter of relative emphasis than hard and fast distinctions between the two. The aim of Chapter 3, which is considerably longer, is to present a case that there can be some preferential features of models of usefulness as compared with theories of truth.

Chapter 4 concludes the book with a short set of conclusions and invitations. You might be inclined to start by checking them over. At any time, I would be delighted if you contacted me to talk over your own notions and ideas on this matter of theories of truth and models of usefulness.

Chapter 2

Distinguishing differences between theories of truth and models of usefulness

Most psychotherapy theorists, researchers, teacher–trainers and practitioners are relatively familiar with what may be called theories of truth, and relatively unfamiliar with what may be called models of usefulness. In this chapter, I am not going to try to define 'model', because that technical word may be used in the philosophy of science. There are probably formal definitions of 'model' in the philosophy of science, but I am not trying to use that word in that particular way.

Instead, I am using the phrase 'models of usefulness' as a kind of conceptual system that differs somewhat from what may be called 'theories of truth' in that: (1) a model of usefulness emphasizes usefulness, i.e. has the virtue of being helpful in accomplishing some defined and explicit aim, goal, use, (2) both the model as a whole and its parts or components are to be understood as convenient fictions, rather than real things and (3) models of usefulness tend to believe in the usefulness of thinking in terms of alternative constructions of events, rather than in some kind of single, grand, underlying truth.

This is what I hope to present as a kind of definition of a model. In this chapter, my aim is to spell out this meaning of 'model', and also to show how theories of truth, and what I am proposing as models of usefulness, can be shown to differ somewhat from each other.

There are at least three reasons why it can be hard to draw some distinguishing differences between theories of truth and models of usefulness. The first is that virtually all reviewers and readers are likely to be proponents of theories of truth. I am arguing on behalf of a constituency that is essentially non-existent. The field of psychotherapy is filled with theories of personality, child development, psychopathology and psychotherapeutic change. It almost seems that the field lacks any respectable alternative to what are referred to as theories (see

Rorty, 1991). It would be easier if at least some reviewers and readers were either somewhat disposed toward either models of usefulness or a distinction between theories of truth and models of usefulness. But that is not the way things are.

The second reason is that the distinguishing differences are more matters of relative emphasis than hard and fast distinctions. Nevertheless, the differences are, I believe, substantial enough to distinguish between the two.

The third reason is that theories of truth and models of usefulness seem to live in quite different worlds, with quite different mind-sets, philosophies and outlooks. It can be deeply challenging for proponents of theories of truth to twist their basic mind-sets sufficiently to appreciate the sheer possibility of models of usefulness. And I do tend to think of them as mind-sets. Long before I had a clear idea of the uses I valued, the goals I valued achieving in a session, I had a kind of vague impression of what I wanted to achieve in a session, and I had a kind of vague impression of what I thought, my way of imagining what human beings were like. My mind-set favored usefulness as more important than ideas of what people were like. I moved from vague and unclear uses and pictures to rather clarified and clear notions of the uses I valued and the pictures that were helpful to have in getting those uses. When I talk seriously with both students and colleagues, I do seem to be talking with mind-sets of either theories of truth or models of usefulness, although there are precious few of the latter.

I therefore expect that most readers are likely to have mind-sets of theories of truth. Nevertheless, I have a kind of naïve trust that most readers can give me a fair opportunity to make a case that there are some differences between what may be regarded as theories of truth and what may be regarded as models of usefulness.

Theories of truth are to be true and models of usefulness are to be useful

Theories of truth are to tell the truth about things, to get as close as possible to the real truth, to provide the best approximation of the truth, to depict the true state of affairs of reality, to tell what things are really like. According to the way that theories of truth see the world, 'the world exists independently of us as knowers, and is the way it is independently of our theoretical knowledge of it. True theories correctly describe that reality' (Chalmers, 1982, p. 147).

You can see whether a theory of truth is any good by seeing if what it says is the truth is really true. This is not the only way of seeing whether a theory of truth is good, but it is an important way.

A theory of truth is to get at the true nature of things, whether it is a theory of personality, a theory of psychopathology or a theory of psychotherapy. The theory is to approximate truth whether it is a theory of gravity, evolution, light, heat or even mathematics:

> The French geometers who constructed the most important theories in mathematical physics had a continual tendency to regard them as true explanations of things and the true causes of phenomena.
>
> Duhem (1996, p. 60)

Models of usefulness are the new kid on the block. Their premium is usefulness. Their justification is mainly that they are useful. They are helpful for some job, to achieve some useful goal, end or task. A 'model is treated as an approximation useful for certain purposes' (Achinstein, 1965, p. 104). The main way of seeing whether a model of usefulness is any good is by seeing whether it indeed is useful, helpful, for the particular job, task or use.

A theory of human development, personality, behavior or cognition tries to get at the truth about those things. A theory of emotions seeks to get at the truth about emotions, at the true nature of emotions, at the true structure and organization of emotions. In contrast, a model looks at things in terms of some use, job or task. Models are more inclined to say, 'If you think of or picture human development or personality or behavior or cognition in this way, then you will be better able to achieve the particular use you have in mind, do that particular job, accomplish that particular aim or goal.' A model of emotions places emphasis on helping you to achieve some particular use such as heightening the emotion, opening up some emotion, freeing the person of some painful emotion.

Both theories of truth and models of usefulness make statements, make pronouncements, say things. Here are three such statements:

1. Depression is usually a consequence of some irrational belief.
2. Depression is a symptom of underlying repressed aggression.

3. To discover the deeper potential for experiencing, it is important to find a scene in which the feeling of depression is strong.

A theory of truth has a mind-set in which the question is: 'Is this statement true, an accurate depiction of what is true about depression?' A model of usefulness has a mind-set in which the question is: 'Is thinking this way helpful in achieving the use I want to achieve?' Models have a different mind-set from theories. 'One does not ask if a knowledge claim is an accurate depiction of the real – is it true? One asks, rather, does acting on this claim produce successful results?' (Polkinghorne, 1992, p. 15; see also Mahoney, 1989).

There are some age-old basic issues and questions. One is what the relationship between the mind and the body is. Another has to do with the relationship between the whole and its parts. Is the whole greater than the sum of its parts? Does the whole determine the role and function of its parts, or do the parts determine the role and function of the whole? Theories tend to vie with one another to come up with the position that is closest to the truth. Theories try to show that they are closer to the truth than rival theories. In contrast, models are much more inclined to ask: 'Which position on this basic issue is more useful for the job I have in mind?' Theories and models do seem to have qualitatively different mind-sets with regard to positions on these age-old basic issues.

The emphasis on approximating truth or on being useful is, indeed, a matter of relative emphasis. Theories do not entirely turn their backs on usefulness, but they place far more emphasis on approximating truth. A theory of truth may be checked out in terms of its usefulness, but the truly important criterion is its approximation of truth. 'That is, we are to judge them not merely by determining whether they are empirically adequate or useful, but also whether they are true or false' (Erwin, 1992, p. 165). In theories of truth, whether they are true or false is the heavier and more valued criterion. In contrast, models of usefulness place almost exclusive emphasis on sheer usefulness.

Models do not even try hard to get at the truth about things, to be true and not false. Whereas theories of truth are forever competing in the struggle to approximate truth, models of usefulness are usually elsewhere engaged, trying to be helpful in the achievement of some use, aim, goal, task or end.

Parts of a theory should be real and true; parts of a model should be useful fictions

A conceptual system is almost always made up of parts, pieces and bits, components. This seems to be the case whether the conceptual system leans toward being a theory or a model. There are usually different kinds of parts.

Some parts are the things of which personality is supposed to be comprised. Open up personality, and there are parts such as egos and superegos, core cognitions, metacognitions, maternal instincts, an unconscious and unconscious impulses, defense mechanisms, effectance motivations, basic needs, growth forces, archetypes, self-defeating thoughts, psychopathological processes, intrapsychic conflicts, primary and secondary process material, repressed memories and affects, rigid supraordinate constructs, introjections and other personality parts.

Some parts are elements of more general notions and ideas about how people come to be the way they are, who and what they are, how and why they change, and what they can become. These include such parts as schizophrenia, borderline conditions, intermittent reinforcements, anal stage of development, transference neuroses, countertransferences, helping relationships, tears in the working alliance, symptom clusters, empathic attunements, contingency respondings, proactive inhibition, addictive personalities, unipolar affect disorders, sexual co-dependencies, loss of transitional objects and paranoid states.

Some parts are in the form of basic principles, postulates, propositions, presumptions and assumptions, dictums, made up of these pieces and bits. Here are just a few:

> Biological, neurological, physiological and chemical events and variables are basic to psychological events and variables.
>
> Human beings have inborn, intrinsic, biological and psychological needs, drives, instincts and motivations.

Some parts are in the form of propositions and principles that are secondary, auxiliary, derived or deduced from the more basic, fundamental, foundational propositions, principles, postulates, dictums, e.g.

> Client expressiveness is a factor in client productivity.

Interruption of the maternal instinctual bonding with the infant is a significant causal determinant of abnormal development.

Theories of truth generally accept that their parts are real and true.
Their personality parts are real and true. There are really and truly
things like egos and metacognitions and growth forces. They exist.
Theories of truth know that the parts that deal with how a person
comes to be the way he or she is, who and what a person is, how and
why a person changes and what a person can become are real and
true. There really and truly are parts such as borderline conditions,
anal stage of development, tears and rips in the helping alliance, schizophrenia and proactive inhibition. They exist. There really are basic
needs, transference neuroses, defense mechanisms and operant condi-
tionings. They exist.

Theories of truth believe in the truth of their basic postulates, fundamental dictums, foundational principles. It is true that biological,
neurological, physiological and chemical events and variables are
basic to psychological events and variables. It is true that the brain is
a basic determinant of human growth and development. It is true that
there are mental illnesses, diseases and disorders. They may be true
because they are simply eternal verities. They may be true because they
are defined as true in basic postulates, i.e. 'definition by postulate'
(Campbell, 1953, p. 290). They may be true because they are self-evident truths, much like the axioms of Euclidian geometry. 'The
foundations of that particular body of knowledge are conceived to be
axioms, statements such as "only one straight line can be drawn join-
ing two points." It can plausibly be said of such axioms that they are
self-evidently true' (Chalmers, 1982, p. 115).

Theories of truth know that their secondary, auxiliary, derived or
deduced principles and propositions are also true, provided that they
are logically derived or deduced from the basic postulates, fundamental dictums, foundational principles, which are of course true. In other
words, 'if the first set is true, then the second set is true' (Campbell,
1953, p. 290), provided that the derivation or deduction was carried
out properly, logically and rigorously.

In contrast, the parts of a model are conceived and understood as
convenient fictions. All of a model's pieces and bits, entities and things
are thought of as convenient fictions, unreal and invented, untrue and
fictitious, but useful tools in helping to get the job done, 'convenient
fictions enabling scientists to relate and make predictions about

observable manifestations' (Chalmers, 1982, p. 146). The premium is on propositions being convenient, helpful, useful, rather than being true or false. As Ariew and Barker (1996, p. xi) say about Duhem's philosophy of science: 'Theoretical propositions are not true or false, but "convenient" or "inconvenient".'

In creating a piece of the model, in including this concept in the model, the question is whether this element is useful. The question is not whether the piece or element is real or true or can be found in nature, e.g. when mathematicians 'construct a model, they make it from materials which seem to them to be the most convenient without ever asking themselves if the arrangements they imagine have the least analogy in nature with the properties that they want to reproduce' (Duhem, 1996, p. 59). If we include a piece called the unconscious or effectance motivation, core construct or deeper potential for experiencing, the important consideration is whether including this invented piece is useful, not whether it truly exists in nature.

Models invent things called 'causes' and 'effects', but models know that these things are convenient fictions. Models believe that the real world contains all sorts of things, events, but none of these things are really causes or effects. Instead, causes and effects are designations that we put on the real things of nature, fictions that models invent, because it is convenient to invent these fictions:

> There is no cause or effect in nature; nature has but an individual existence; nature simply *is*. Recurrences of like cases in which A is always connected to B, that is like results under like circumstances, that is, again, the essence of the connection of cause and effect, exist but in the abstraction which we perform for the purpose of mentally reproducing the facts.
>
> Mach (1960, p. 580)

Nature contains no causes and effects; models invent causes and effects because they are convenient fictions.

In models, the parts of 'personality' are conveniently useful fictions, providing helpful pictures – picture consciousness in terms of tiny particles that have to reach a certain size in order to ring the bell of conscious awareness. Picture a psychoanalytic personality system in terms of a plumbing metaphor. Picture the experiential personality system in terms of a limited number of circles, each representing an individualized potential for experiencing, with some circles being lower or deeper than others, and all of the potentials for experiencing relating to one another in a positive or negative relationship. Picture cognitive schemas and maternal instincts, unconscious wishes and effectance motivations, repressed memories and dependency needs. All of these personality parts are thought of as convenient fictions. None of these personality parts is thought of as real and true.

In models, the parts dealing with how a person comes to be, how a person is, how change occurs and what a person can be are thought of as convenient fictions. These parts can be framed as pictures or statements, propositions, but they and what they refer to are merely convenient fictions – useful but not thought of as real and true.

In models, basic principles, fundamental starting points and foundational beliefs are all conceived as convenient fictions, useful ways of thinking of things, basic and foundational things, but not as basic truths. Foundational beliefs are simply beliefs, useful for the enterprise that you have in mind, whether the enterprise is small and pocket-sized or grandiose, such as human beings becoming free of painful feelings and painful situations and also becoming the kinds of human beings they are capable of becoming. Change the use or enterprise and you probably have to fabricate a new bunch of foundational beliefs:

> ... postulates cannot be regarded as simply formal statements of general assumptions. Since postulates are set up for different sorts of enterprises, they necessarily vary as the enterprises vary.
>
> Kantor (1945, p. 1)

In models, all of their parts are invented, carefully conceived and organized. But they are not thought of as real and true. Instead, they are thought of as conveniently useful fictions, hypothetical constructs (Whitehead, 1929, MacCorquodale and Meehl, 1948, Mahrer, 1989, 1996/2004). 'They are not . . . to be proved or disproved, but are convenient representations of things' (Skinner, 1938, p. 44). They are convenient because, if you think in terms of these parts, you can be helped to achieve the use you want to achieve (see van Fraassen, 1980, 1989, Rotgers, 1988).

In theories of truth, constructs may be used that refer to things that are hypothesized to be true but may not currently be reducible to the observable. These constructs refer to things such as the unconscious, basic needs or conditioning, each of which is hypothesized as true. These constructs 'assert the existence of entities and the occurrence of events not reducible to the observable' (MacCorquodale and Meehl, 1948, p. 105). In contrast, models invent or create all sorts of constructs, including the unconscious basic needs, or conditioning, each of which is unabashedly presented as unreal fictions, none of which assert the existence of entities or the occurrence of actual events, each of which is invented because it is helpful, convenient and useful to invent them.

In theories of truth, all the various kinds of parts are to be real and true. The parts of personality are real and true. Basic dictums are to be true. In models of usefulness, all of the various kinds of parts are there, but they are convenient fictions, effectively and neatly useful ways to think of things. The parts of personality are invented, made up, fictitious, but deliciously useful to conceive of. Foundational beliefs are no more than beliefs, notions, ideas, fictions, useful places to start.

Theories of truth believe in a single underlying truth; models of usefulness believe in alternative constructions of events

Theories of truth deal with things that are real and true. These things have an underlying true nature and content, an underlying true structure and organization. Theories are made to get as close as possible to the way things truly are, the true nature of things, the single underlying truth that is correct, accurate, veridical (Honer and Hunt, 1987, Leahey, 1991, Richards and Bergin, 1997, Viney and King, 1998). Nature is not random or haphazard, unknowable or capriciously whimsical, forever beyond reasoned and researched understanding. Nature is not whatever a person thinks it is or paints it to be. Instead, there is an underlying order and structure to nature. There are knowable laws governing nature. Once our theories get at the underlying truth about nature, we can predict and control nature.

Theories of truth believe in a single underlying truth to things such as an emotion of anger, competitive behavior, schizophrenia, irrational cognitions. When we know the truth, we know what these things really are, how these things really work, the laws that govern them, their underlying structure, content, nature and organization. There is a single underlying truth to the things in the world of psychotherapy, and it is the mission of theories of truth to know what that truth is and what makes anger tick, how to predict and control competitive behavior, what schizophrenia is all about, and the true nature and structure of irrational cognitions.

In contrast, models of usefulness believe that there can be events out there that may be real and true, but they are mere events. Models of usefulness believe that these events are marvelously open to descriptive words and phrases, to alternative kinds of descriptions and constructions. They believe that an exceedingly sharp distinction can be drawn between these alternative descriptions or constructions and the actual events to which they refer, the mere events that the descriptions describe and the constructs construct. That thing out there may be concretely real and true, but it is nicely open to descriptive words and constructs such as white, ceramic, cup, an emotion of anger, competitive behavior, a borderline state or an irrational cognition. Each of these words and phrases is understood as quite different from the mere event that these words and phrases refer to.

Models of usefulness believe that, whereas events are open to alternative systems of description and construction, some of these alternative systems may be more useful and others less useful for particular purposes. If I seek to have something to drink from, describing that event as white or ceramic may not be as useful as describing it as a cup. If I seek to enable the person to become the deeper person that she is capable of becoming, describing it as some kind of deeper potential for experiencing is likely to be more useful than describing it as white, ceramic, a cup or a borderline mental illness. Models of usefulness believe in alternative constructions of events, each of which may be reasonably justified, but some of which are probably more useful than others.

The intention of this chapter has been to draw a serious but somewhat soft distinction between what may be called theories of truth and models of usefulness. In the field of psychotherapy, my impression is that almost all of the conceptual systems may be stamped as theories of truth, and that few if any of the conceptual systems genuinely qualify as models of usefulness. The intention of Chapter 3 is to make a case for the field of psychotherapy to acknowledge some useful features of models of usefulness, and to reserve a little room for them, if only as friendly complements to the much more popular theories of truth.

Chapter 3

Some preferential features of models of usefulness over theories of truth

This is probably going to be a hard sell because I tend to believe that almost all readers think in terms of theories of truth, and I am going to try to make a case in favor of some ways in which models of usefulness have advantages, preferences, over theories of truth. I do have some serious misgivings and doubts about being able to get a fair hearing from many readers.

Perhaps it might help to try to clarify the main point I hope to make. I am not advocating that the field of psychotherapy replace its theories with models. I am not saying that theories are bad, models are good. My point is that there are some particular ways in which models of usefulness are indeed better than, or preferable to, theories of truth. My hope is that the field can at least consider reserving a little room for models of usefulness, just a little room, when their features qualify them as preferable to theories of truth. My hope is that there will be times when the field will find it preferable to use a model rather than a theory. My hope is that the field will at least acknowledge that its conceptual systems include both theories of truth and some models of usefulness.

My own experiential conceptual system is a wholesale, out and out, thoroughgoing model (Mahrer, 1989, 1996/2004). I am exceedingly aware that what follows is an attempt by a dedicated model proponent to try to convince proponents of theories that the field can benefit from having room for both.

Models are especially useful in providing pictori-alized conceptualizations to help get the job done

Suppose that you have some job in mind, some change you want to bring about, some use you want to achieve. Models are built on the idea that, if you think this way, have this mind-set or have this pictorial conceptualization, then you can more easily achieve that use than if you think that way, adopt that other mind-set or hold that other pictorial conceptualization. If you want to achieve that job or use, it helps if you adopt this pictorialized conceptualization, this model, of how people are, what people are like, how a person gets to be the way he or she is, what a person can become, what changes can occur and how they can occur.

Models are exceedingly job-oriented (see Toulman, 1953). If you want to enable this person to become a whole new person, the person this person is capable of becoming, and if you want to achieve this in one session, it helps you to think of people in this way, as changing in this way, as able to become like this if you adopt this model. The model need not be true, or portray the way people truly are, but it works, it helps you to achieve the use you intended to achieve.

A theory of emotions is geared to tell what is true about how many primary emotions there are, what these emotions are, the truth about their structure and organization, and how they are related to metacognitions and behavior. In contrast, a model is more helpful in some uses that you want to achieve with emotions. If you think this way about emotions, here are ways to bring them forward, heighten their strength or to become free of some painful emotion in some scene. The model merely strives to be useful. It does not strive to identify the emotion as primary or secondary, or get at the true structure and organization of emotions.

I was having trouble opening the front door of the house that my friend had asked me to check while she was in Brazil. The key went into the keyhole all right, but I could not unlock the door. 'I can show you how to open the door.' My 'helper' was serious, and about six or seven years old. She explained to me how keys and locks work. The key is to jiggle the lock, to make it happy, to tickle the lock. Then the lock opens. You have to put the key in and then jiggle it and wiggle it to tickle the lock. I tried her pictorialized model. It worked. My theory of tumblers and such was not especially useful. Two days later I again went to my friend's home. I made sure that I used the little lady's model of keys and locks. It worked.

My aim is to become more and more of the person I am capable of becoming. I also want to become free of the painful scenes in my personal world, and the painful feelings in those painful scenes. I know that these two ambitious aims fit with some sort of notion or idea about who and what I am and can be, but they were important aims for me. I spent many years trying hard to find a way of thinking about and picturing what a person is like, what makes up a person, how a person gets to be the person that he or she is, how and why people do the things they do and feel the way they feel, what people can become, how change can take place, how and why people are the way they are with one another.

I was not trying to find the real answers to these questions, to get at the supposed truth. I wanted to arrive at a way of answering these basic questions, of picturing human beings, that was marvelously helpful and useful in achieving those two magnificent aims. I now have a model of how a person comes about in the first place, of how a person becomes the person he or she is, of how change occurs, of answers to all those basic questions (Mahrer, 1989, 1996/2004). It is a pictorial model that is excitingly useful in enabling me to attain my two precious aims. It is not a theory of what is true.

My pictorialized model of a human being is merely a useful picture, a useful model. It is intended to be useful. It is not intended to be an accurate depiction of the personality structure of a person. In my picture, there are circles representing 'potentials for experiencing' even though I do not believe that if you open up human beings you will find circular things with 'potential for experiencing' labels on them. If I constructed a model that you can touch, paint and take apart, it would be an apparatus that is useful in simulating the phenomena with which I deal. It would not be an accurate depiction of the phenomena. 'Even when he is writing a paper on the constitution of the aether or of matter, W. Thompson never forgets that he is not laying hold of the essence of things. He confines himself to constructing an apparatus capable of simulating certain phenomena' (Duhem, 1996, p. 61). The aim is to construct a pictorialized conceptualization that can help get the job done. That is all.

Helping to get the job done: the primary aim for models, a secondary aim for theories of truth

Models are born and bred to be useful in getting some jobs done. This is their bread and butter, their strong suit, their reason for being. Models ought to be useful because that is their primary purpose, their essential use.

Compared with models of usefulness, theories place relatively less emphasis on simple, practical, sheer usefulness. Theories of truth are not thought of as useless, but as less useful than models. For theories of truth, usefulness is a secondary virtue. Their primary virtue is approximating what is true. Indeed, the usefulness of theories depends on their first being true. A theory 'is useful *because* it is "true" or, put in nonabsolutist terms, it is useful because it is a relatively more accurate reflection . . . of reality' (Speed, 1984, p. 513).

Which precedes which?

Once you figure out the theory, you can think of its practical applications, versus the valued use precedes conceptualization of how and why it works. It seems relatively easy and relatively safe to hold that there is a back-and-forth interaction between a practical application and use, on the one hand, and conceptualizing how and why something works, on the other. But that is not the question. Rather, the question is 'Which seems to have the first big push?' You can believe that first you figure out the basic theory; then you can figure out its practical applications. Or you can believe that first there is a valued use, a practical use, and then there is an effort to figure out how and why it works.

Proponents of theories of truth are inclined to think in terms of the development and establishment of the theory of truth, the basic and fundamental theory of truth. Then you can figure out the more practical applications, the applied uses. Proponents of models of usefulness tend to go in the opposite direction. First there is a valuing of the actual use, the tinkering with and improvement of the actual use. This seems to occur before attempts at what might be called high-level conceptualization of how and why it works.

For example, a few thousand years ago the use of dreams as ways of foretelling the future or as indications of what was deep inside was relatively well advanced before the development of sophisticated conceptualizations of how and why dreams could be, and indeed were, used in these ways. A case can be made that it was the actual use of dreams that was an effective launching pad for conceptualization. How could dreams foretell the future? How could dreams reveal what was deeper inside? Conceptualizations followed, and they consisted of speculations about messages from the gods or speculations about reduced ego defenses during sleep, rather than these conceptualizations that somehow existed in free conceptual space, and some bright people thinking, 'If gods transmitted their messages while people slept, then maybe dreams just might be used to foretell the future' or, 'If ego defenses are reduced during sleep, maybe dreams might be used to get at a person's unconscious impulses'.

One mind-set is that first a theory of truth is developed, then we can look for some practical applications and uses of this theory of truth. A different mind-set is that some practical use is valued, and this is carried forward; there are then conceptualizations of how and why it works.

Grand truths and grand practical applications, versus the breadth and depth of the use

Theories can set their sights on what is referred to as 'basic', answering fundamental questions such as the basic differences between the organic and the inorganic, and what is living and non-living matter. Theories can strive to make grand pronouncements on basic issues, such as the differences between the mind and the body, and whether human behavior is caused by genetics, the environment or some combination. Theories can set out to answer eternal questions about human nature and set forth eternal verities.

Once theories can find the basic truths, they can look for practical applications, which can be grand and have impressive breadth and depth because the basic truths are broad and deep.

Models start from the intended or hoped-for uses. These uses may be broad and deep or narrow and shallow. They may consist of enabling people to undergo radical and deep-seated qualitative transformation or to increase the reading rate by a few percentage points in high-achieving high school students in the local community.

The breadth and depth of the use go a long way to determining the breadth and depth of the model. If the use is narrow and shallow, the conceptual model may well be narrow and shallow. If the use is broad and deep, the conceptual model may also be broad and deep, and can deal with issues that are broad and deep, the eternal questions about human beings.

Conceptual understanding of the phenomenon: the bonus of models of how to get the job done

Theories of truth rarely speak directly about models. However, theories of truth speak indirectly about a science in which models might be relegated to secondary and inferior status. They talk about a distinction between rather practical and down-to-earth 'cookbook science' and the more sophisticated and elevated 'explanatory science' (Gale, 1979), or between a low-level science of 'knowing how' to do something and a loftier science of 'knowing that or why' something is the case (Ryle, 1949). In other words, theories of truth often create a landscape in which models might be equipped to do the more inferior work, but cannot do the loftier, elevated, superior conceptual work.

Models do not think in the same way as theories of truth. They do say that they can enable users to get the job done, to achieve the use, whether or not this is called 'cookbook science' or 'knowing how' to do something. Models also say that their pictorial models offer conceptualizations of the phenomenon in question, conceptualizations that may well be elevated, lofty and sophisticated. In other words, models cheerfully and dedicatedly do both.

Theories of truth generally claim that they get at the truth of some phenomena, that they emphasize the 'basic' stuff. They study dreams and the pupil of the eye. Once we know more about the truth of dreams and the pupil of the eye, we can turn our attention to the 'applied' use of that 'basic' knowledge. Theories are basic and their findings can be of use in applied work.

Models of use can also do both, but in reverse order. If the applied use is to help bring about deep-seated personal change, models can be helpful in making sense of how and why dreams can be useful. If dreams are found to be helpful in this or that way, models can offer a pictorial representation, a conceptual model, of the phenomenon of dreams and dreaming. In other words, models can be both applied and basic. Models not only can show how to get the job done, they can also provide conceptual understanding of the phenomenon.

Simplified pictorializations of models and complicated conceptual systems of theories

A friend of mine happened to do a review of my book that presented my experiential model of human beings (Mahrer, 1989), and later a review of my book that included a model of psychotherapeutic change (Mahrer, 1996/2004). He told me that my models must be wrong because they were so simple. They fit on a single page, a single diagram or picture, a single page of text with some paragraphs of explanatory notes. In contrast, although most theories could be boiled down to a page or so, even a working appreciation of most theories required a substantial number of pages to justify the complicated conceptual systems that represent most theories. With a fair amount of reading and reflection, it did seem that models come with the virtue of simplification, even of simplicity, compared with most theories. Why?

One reason may be that a model simplifies, distills or represents a great deal of complicated conceptualizations in a single, and simple, picture, diagram or equation:

> It is rather paradoxical to realise that when a picture, a drawing, a diagram is called a model for a physical system, it is for the same reason that a formal set of postulates is called a model for a physical system. This reason can be indicated in one word: simplification. The mind needs in one act to have an overview of the essential characteristics of a domain; therefore the domain is represented either by a set of equations or by a picture or by a diagram.
>
> Apostel (1961, p. 15)

A second reason why most theories are apparently much more complicated, extensive and complex than models is that the basic principles, axioms, fundamental dictums, postulates and assumptions of most theories are regarded as truths, not as conveniently useful fictions. As they are true, logical reasoning can generate a whole complicated latticework of secondary or deduced statements of truth. Provide a mathematician with a small set of truths, and an extensive system can be generated. In theories, if we start with these basic truths, we can logically generate a complicated conceptual system of subsequent truths. In models, there are simply foundational beliefs, convenient fictions, not basic truths containing the seeds of hundreds of logically generated subsequent truths.

A third reason why most theories are usually far more complicated conceptual systems than most models is that theories, if they are any good, are expected to offer good explanations, accounts, predictions and understandings of what the theories are theories of. A theory of behavior or social change or psychopathology is faced with a bewildering array of things for which it is supposed to provide the true explanation and understanding. A theory of human behavior faces an almost overwhelming and unending sea of challenges. How can you explain this and that behavior, how this particular behavior comes about, why only some people behave this or that way, how this behavior changes or does not change, and on and on? In almost stark contrast, most models limit their claims to helping to accomplish this particular job. Nothing more. It never promised to provide the true explanation and accounting for all those events. That is not the job of a model.

For better or worse, most models have the feature of simplification, whereas most theories are more inclined toward consisting of far more complicated conceptual systems.

Comparatively greater openness of models to improvement and replacement

In general, psychotherapy has not especially distinguished itself with a proud track record of continually advancing or improving its theories, or giving them up in favor of better ones (Quine, 1969, 1974, Siegel, 1996). It seems that most theories come equipped with a substantial inertia, a built-in resistance to change. Once a theory is set, it tends to remain essentially set. In relative contrast, models of usefulness seem almost to come with a naïvely friendly openness to modification, improvement or even replacement with more useful ones. Models welcome improvement; theories growl at being tinkered with. Models welcome replacement; theories have a primitive fear of dying.

In the course of sheer living, it is easy to develop entrenched theories of what people are like; in contrast, models are more like helpful tools for particular jobs

Over the course of childhood and adulthood, both before and after professional training, most people have worked out some rather well-entrenched notions of how people get to be the way they are, how and why people seem to be similar to or different from one another, what seems to make a person feel good or bad, why it is that people seem to see things differently, what kinds of people to move toward or away from, why it is that some people seem better or worse off than others, how and why some people do things that seem weird, kind of scary, hard to fathom, crazy, bizarre. Over the first few decades of living, most people are likely to have developed theories of human beings that are exceedingly entrenched. These theories have been fashioned and put to the test hundreds or thousands of times over the course of sheer living. These theories or 'folk psychologies' (Stich, 1983, Fodor, 1987, Furnham, 1987, Place, 1996) have developed powerful roots that tend to lock them in place.

As a result, sheer living seems to help entrench some sort of theory of what human beings are like, but not such entrenched theories of particle resistance, orbital curvature or thermonuclear inversion. Furthermore, over the course of a lifetime, it is likely that a person will tend to have a single, grand metatheory, rather than several competing rival theories.

In contrast, models of usefulness are typically more lightweight, less entrenched, more tied to particular tasks, jobs or uses. They are more like helpful tools for particular jobs. Rather than coalescing into one grand megatool, it is far easier to generate different tools for different jobs, different models for different uses. Even if a person becomes fond of a particular model, it can be easier to acknowledge that there are indeed other models around, and some may well be more useful for this or for that particular purpose. In general, models are much less entrenched than theories.

Basic, eternal, immutable truths or clarification of the job to be done?

When a theory is being conceived, first being framed, it is common to start by defining its basic truths, its fundamental starting points, what it takes for granted as true, its assumptions, presumptions, basic principles, axioms, foundational dictums. Theories generally start by a sober setting forth of what it holds as basic and fundamental about human beings, human nature, epistemology, how the world is and works, life. Theories tend to be conceived in rooted basics, and are therefore rather resistant to change, modification or improvement right from the beginning.

Models have virtually no such anchorage, no laying out of a hard cement foundation. Instead, they tend to start with an eye on just what the job to be done is, on defining and clarifying the aim, purpose, goal, intent, job or use. When models start out, they are not fixed in a hard-and-fast foundation, whereas theories are much more inclined to be fixed.

Theories of truth first spell out their basic, fundamental truths; then they can understand and explain things by reasoning from their basic, fundamental truths, e.g. in physics, a theoretician:

> . . . presents a certain number of hypotheses which define the most important, essential, and elementary properties of matter for them. Then, from these fundamental hypotheses, they seek to deduce the explanation of all the phenomena of physics through a logically connected chain of precise deductions . . . Taking as foundations a certain number of very simple postulates, they aspire to deduce from them the explanation of the material world, down to the last detail.
>
> Duhem (1996, p. 61)

Models do not lay out a set of basic and fundamental postulates or truths. Their attention, instead, is focused on the job that is to be done. Theories of truth go about deducing explanations. Models of usefulness are busy trying to get the job done, to achieve the task, to do the work.

When I started out, my vague aim was to make sense of or to know more about this field of psychotherapy. Those who followed theories told me to start with the basic truths in psychotherapy. Socrates told me to start with these basic truths, and then to do my best to reason carefully. That was hard for me because I had big trouble finding and being sure of my basic truths. In 1620, when I talked with Francis Bacon, he asked me what particular phenomenon I was interested in. I told him that I was interested in wonderful changes that happened in what was called psychotherapy, though I was not very clear about what wonderful changes I had in mind. He suggested that I get as close as I could to the phenomenon I was interested in, and to start there (Bacon, 1889). Theorists generally start with the basic truths; proponents of models generally start from the naïve phenomenon in which they are interested.

I talked with people who framed new psychotherapies, who laid out psychoanalytic therapy, bioenergetic therapy, social-learning therapy or cognitive therapy. How did they begin in setting out to frame their psychotherapy? Almost everyone said that they started with truths. Some of these truths were basic and some were more like rules or little truths about how to change the ways that patients thought, what 'personality' was like, the nature of psychopathology, and so on.

I didn't. I started by trying to be as clear as I could about just what I wanted to achieve, about the task, the job. I tried to clarify what the job was. After a while, I was reasonably satisfied that I had two goals. One was to become a qualitatively whole new person, and the other was to be free of scenes of painful feelings. I started by framing out the task, the job. I followed what models advised me to start with. That made more sense to me than starting with what theories advised me to start with.

My colleague holds a theory of truth. When she is asked to say what her theory is, what her approach is, she can say that her approach is cognitive–behavioral. She can even go ahead and spell out some of the general notions of her cognitive–behavioral approach. If I am asked what my theory is, what my approach is, my preferred way of answering is to say that I am drawn toward whatever set of ideas, whatever conceptual system, is especially useful in helping me to attain the two goals or aims or uses that I hold dear. I start with my uses, not with a body of general propositions or truths.

The creator of a grand theory, or a significant departure from some grand theory, is almost forced to stake out its position on what is taken as basic issues, on things like epistemology. The judge asks, 'What is your position on epistemology? Is there a real world independent of a person or of people? Did stars exist before there were people? How do you come to know the real world?' The grand theorist must be clear in stating the new theory's formal position. Thankfully, the newly created constructivist approaches have crafted out a clarified position:

> While there are a variety of constructivist models, they all hold in common the epistemological belief that a totally objective reality, one that stands apart from the knowing subject, can never be fully known [and that] knowledge, and the meaning we imbue it with, is a construction of the human mind.
>
> Rosen (1996, p. 5)

Theories must tell the truth. They tend to start by telling their positions on the grand basic issues of truth. Models do not. Models tend to start by telling about the jobs, aims or uses that they are for. When models tell about their conceptualizations, it is more in the spirit of 'here are some of the basic beliefs' rather than 'here is my position of what is true on this basic issue of what is true'. For example, I have a fairly clear position on the above issue about a real world and knowing the real world. However, first, my position was arrived at long after the model was developed – I did not start with it – second, my position is only a convenient belief, not a position of truth (Mahrer, 1989), and therefore considers the problem of which position is supposedly true to be a wholesomely illusory problem (Mahrer, 1995b) and, third, my position is eminently modifiable and not at all an eternal verity. When I first outlined my experiential model, I could easily have bypassed trying to figure out my position on this issue. Theories of truth do not usually have that luxury.

Fundamental order and lawfulness of nature: theory versus model

Most theories accept a basic truth that there is a fundamental order and lawfulness to the world, the universe and nature. This is a basic truth when we are talking about celestial bodies in motion, light and heat, electricity, volcanoes erupting, birth and death, the construction of bridges and buildings, or the structure of atoms and molecules.

In the field of psychotherapy, theories of truth likewise accept the basic truth that there is a fundamental order and lawfulness to human nature, our actions and interactions, the way we think and the way we feel, the way we become who we are and the way we are in groups and communities, the way we love and the way we fight. Our theories of truth search for the underlying order and lawfulness to human nature. We pride ourselves in formulating our laws of effect just as other theories take pride in formulating their laws of thermodynamics.

Models think of this statement as just another foundational belief, rather than a basic truth: 'There is a fundamental order and lawfulness to human nature.' Theories of truth think of this statement as a fundamental truth; models of usefulness think of this statement as a foundational belief. This is a big difference, which makes for a big difference in that models of usefulness reserve the right either to accept or to decline this statement, this proposition, this foundational belief. They can do this depending on whether or not the foundational belief is useful in the model's work, its reason for being, its purpose or aim. Theories of truth have far less freedom to accept or to decline this basic proposition.

Unconstrained, wilder, less reality bound, or to stay closer to the truth?

Thinking of a new or modified theory is almost implicitly bound and constrained by what is the accepted truth. It is as if theories have one foot planted in generally accepted truths. Theories tend to avoid straying too far from their anchoring foundation of basic truths. What is the relationship between the whole and its parts? To venture into creating a new theory or to modify the current theory substantially, it is easy to be reassuringly anchored in what research says or what is already known. To venture that the whole is greater than the sum of its parts, one usually feels reassured if framing this theory is consistent with what is already known.

Models generally do not have such anchors or limits or boundaries. They are freer to be whimsical, silly, frolicking, playful, outrageous. Models have much less constraint, are much less anchored or restricted by what research has pronounced as true or what the field accepts as fundamentally true. Models can range more widely, more freely. Models can explore other whole domains, foreign territories, and do so without guilt about violating constraints, truths or realities. They can add new notions or ideas on the grounds that they help achieve the task, that they work in getting the job done. In adding new notions or ideas, models are not especially constrained by what the field accepts as known, true, established. Models risk violating what theories of truth respect as established knowledge, e.g. Maxwell simply added a new notion or idea of 'flux of displacement' to the electrodynamic equations of his model, and did so without first checking with established knowledge, with established theory, without seeing whether he was violating the established laws of physics:

> Maxwell studies the transformation of the equations of electrody-namics in their own terms, most often without seeking to see behind his transformations the coordination of physical laws. He studies them as one examines the movements of a mechanism. This is why it is a futile effort to seek behind these equations a philosophical idea which is not there.
>
> Duhem (1996, p. 60)

Models are inclined to be more risky, to try out and to incorporate new ideas, without being constrained by what the field considers as established knowledge.

An outlandish new idea has a hard time being welcomed by those whose mind-set is theories of truth. In this mind-set, there is an anchor for what is supposedly already known for sure. If an outlandish new idea violates what is already known, that idea is declared to be out-landish and will probably be rejected: 'this idea has to make sense in terms of what we already know; an outlandish idea is much less like-ly to be right if it contradicts our current knowledge about the world' (Dunbar, 1995, p. 30). Theories of truth tend to be conservative, to hold tight against serious and fundamental change, to resist significant new ideas and ways of thinking.

This is not so in models of usefulness. The test of an idea is whether it works, whether it helps get the job done. There is, accordingly, much greater openness and welcoming of outlandish ideas because the test is usefulness, not whether it violates what theories know as basically true.

Creative new ways and means or loyalty to the tried and true?

Theories are inclined to have relatively ingrained and accepted aims and goals, and they are inclined to develop ways and means of accom-plishing these aims and goals because they work and make good sense in terms of what is already known. Accordingly, in most therapies, therapists and clients spend most of their time attending to one anoth-er over the course of the session. This is standard, accepted, and theories would be inclined to stay with the tried and true. It is rather unlikely that a number of theorists would come up with a grossly different scenario in which therapists and clients attended mainly to some third center of attention throughout the session.

To a larger extent than theories, models tend to respect and value the task, the intended aim or goal of the work. When the user of a model works backward, there is a much greater readiness and willingness to welcome exciting, new, creative ways and means, and a readiness and willingness to depart from and to let go of the tried and true. If some new method might do the trick, let's use it; if that means abandoning the established method, the standard and accepted method, the tried and true, then by all means let us do so.

The model user may reason along these lines: my aim, in this single session, is to enable the person to become the qualitatively new person that he is capable of becoming, wholesale transformation, and also for the new person to be free of the painful scene, and the painful feelings in the scene, which was front and center at the start of the session. I believe that, to accomplish this aim, the person has to start with a scene of powerful feeling, and must actually live and be in that exceedingly alive and real scene. My search for how to accomplish this has come up with a particular method in which the attention of both the person and the therapist is fully deployed in the detailed specifics of that scene of strong feeling and of actually living and being in the immediate scene itself. This particular method works. It is an apparently new method. It also seems to mean letting go of the commonplace method in which therapists and clients spend most of their time mainly attending to one another (Mahrer, 2002a, 2002b, Mahrer and Johnston, 2002).

By starting with their intended aims, models tend to favor finding and using creative new ways and means. By respecting what they accept as true, theories tend to remain more loyal to tried and true methods.

Modification: avoidance or acceptance?

If some supreme judge says that the theory has to be modified, the theory is usually not very happy about this. It means that something about the theory is probably wrong, false, untrue. That is often hard to take because the theory tends to pride itself on being true, and on its important parts being true. After all, theories of truth are to have rock-solid foundations made up of basic truths, eternal verities, self-evident truths, assumptions that can be counted on as true. If they are admitted to be untrue, the whole world crumbles, the entire foundation falls apart, and the world of lawful, ordered regularity is replaced by disorder, bedlam and chaos.

On paper, theories ought to welcome being shown to be wrong, false, to have failed. At least, this is what Popper says (1972a, 1972b, 1980). If a theory is shown to be wrong, false, a failure, 'the scientific failure can be fed back into the theory responsible for it, thereby giving us a chance to improve it' (Bunge, 1972, p. 75, see Chalmers, 1982, Bartley, 1988). However sensible this sounds, theories rarely welcome submission to the embarrassment of being publicly shown to be wrong, false, a failure. Theories, in other words, seem to have a built-in resistance to being changed, altered, modified.

In stark contrast, if the supreme judge pronounces the model's basic beliefs to be mere beliefs, not truths, the model not only can smile and say 'I know', but can even welcome modifying its convenient fictions, its foundational beliefs, in order to provide greater service, to be more useful. If the model includes a convenient fiction of an 'ego', we can keep the trusty eye on actual usefulness, and ask some telling questions: 'Does this notion of "ego" really help me in my in-session work? Do I actually use this notion of "ego" in my in-session work? If I actually let go of this notion of "ego", will my in-session work suffer?' If the answer is no to these and other related questions, I have a chance of perhaps modifying this notion of ego. I can even let it go.

If a theory dares to find out that it is not true, or that some of its important parts are not true, the theory is entitled to be embarrassed, to feel second rate, inadequate. In contrast, a model may happily turn itself inside out, throw out and replace lots of its parts, if that would help make the modified model more useful.

Theories are generally supposed to be approximations of the truths, and the rule is supposed to be that a good theory politely makes way for a better theory. That is how science is supposed to work. In other words, 'one may, without contradiction, consider a theory good and propose to replace it with a better theory' (Duhem, 1996, p. 10). But that is not especially how things work in psychotherapy. Proponents of a theory are inclined to have faith in their theory, to believe it to be the truth, rather than a mere approximation of truth. Accordingly, it is rare that proponents say out loud: 'Our theory is good, but we are ready to replace it with this other theory, which is a better theory.

Therefore we are replacing cognitive theory with existential theory, because we acknowledge that existential theory is better.'

If the grand creator of a grand theory actually revises the theory in some significant way, that act can be an almost devastating blow to proponents who regard the theory as a hallowed and revered revelation, a momentous creation from on high. A grand theory is the revelation of truth. If the grand creator has to modify the theory, it now seems that the creator is all too human, not God-like, is flawed, an ordinary theoretician with ordinary faults. If a person has the effrontery to dare modify someone else's grand theory, that person should first show that she or he has earned the elevated qualities that grant one that special right to ascend the high plateau and to modify what has been revealed as the grand truth.

In contrast, proponents of models tend to have an altogether different mind-set. Once a model is fully sculpted out, there is a kind of naïvely hopeful expectation that it will be further developed, it will continue evolving, altering, modifying, changing, improving. My models of human beings (Mahrer, 1989) and psychotherapy (Mahrer, 1996/2004) are mere belief systems ready for modification, but not for devoted commitment. In this sense, proponents of models agree with what Lakatos (1976, p. 205) wrote about Popper: '*Belief* may be a regrettably unavoidable biological weakness to be kept under the control of criticism; but *commitment* is for Popper an outright crime.'

To question or not to question foundational beliefs?

Models tend to regard their foundational beliefs as mere beliefs, not as basic truths. Their foundational beliefs are relatively friendly and lightweight. They are more useful and helpful than they are true. They can be tinkered and played with. They can be called fictions and illusions because they are. There are really no such things as schizophrenia or cognitive schemas, gods or egos, laws of human nature or a basic drive toward aggression.

Nor is there, in models, any superstructure or authorities to pronounce these foundational beliefs as basic truths, eternal verities, a cumulative body of knowledge. Authorities do not dress foundational beliefs in the robes of basic truths. There is no system of teachers and supervisors to inculcate each generation of students into saluting the basic truths. There is no administration, no bureaucracy, no bible, no required examination, to raise the level of foundational beliefs into hallowed truths, ingrained truths, system-approved basic truths.

However, when those who hold to models dare to question what theories of truth hold dear, what theories of truth worship as foundational truths, it is no longer a game. Now things can be deadly serious. Those who hold to models are now opposed by the authorities, the establishment, by all those who made those foundational beliefs into hallowed truths, into facts. Basic facts do not become basic facts all by themselves. They need to be stamped as basic facts by the important people in the field, by the authorities.

> In other words, facts achieve their status through a social process . . . claims do not become facts unless an authority gives them a promotion. The more powerful people supporting a claim, the harder the fact becomes, and the more likely it is that the fact becomes institutionalized.
>
> Lerum (1998, p. 26, see Latour, 1987)

You may be permitted to question, even to tinker with, what for you are foundational beliefs. However, when these are authority-promoted foundational truths, the cornerstones of what is eternally true, the basic axioms of what we should all bow down to as the laws of human nature, when these are written in their textbooks, their final examination and their cumulative body of knowledge, you had better watch out. You will be trivialized, forced to recant, burned at the stake, punished, excommunicated, distanced and hidden away. The entire system will be galvanized into opposing you.

Theories establish criteria of what makes a theory a good one. One of these relatively common criteria is that there is to be a substantial goodness of fit with generally accepted foundational truths and metaphysical positions (Newton-Smith, 1981). If a candidate, new theory violates this criterion, it is in real danger of being rejected. However, this does not especially hold in regard to models. There is no such criterion of the worth of a model. In the world of models, there is little or no emphasis on what theories refer to as generally accepted foundational truths, generally accepted metaphysical positions. This criterion may well apply to theories, but not especially to models.

Models can and do allow their foundational beliefs to be scrutinized, challenged, played with and even altered and replaced. Theories have good reason for being threatened and outraged. The entire system will probably be aroused into seriously defending itself and attacking you if you dare to question its foundational truths.

To switch or not to switch mind-sets?

A mind-set is a whole new way of thinking, a whole new perspective or way of understanding things. It is being able to switch from thinking that the sun revolves around the earth to thinking in terms of the earth revolving around the sun, from thinking that the earth is flat to thinking of the earth as round. It is being able to argue in favor of abortion and switch fully and deeply into arguing against abortion.

The common mind-set holds that psychotherapy is treating a client's personal problems, psychological difficulties, diagnostic illness or disorder, an application of psychotherapeutic methods, the establishment of a helpful therapist–client relationship and working in some psychotherapeutic approach or theory or orientation. A whole different mind-set is that psychotherapy is just another context in which a person can undergo important personal feelings and experiences, that both the person in the role of therapist and the person in the role of client are gaining important personal feelings and experiences from being with one another.

Are you able to switch whole mind-sets, to hold one mind-set fully and passionately and then switch to a rival, alternative mind-set? In general, doing this is relatively hard for those whose mind-set is a theory of truth, and is comparatively easier for those whose mind-set is a model of usefulness.

A better way of achieving the use in model and theory change

Models arise from actual, real, demonstrated uses. Models stake their worth on being useful. If a proponent of a particular model is shown that some other way is much more effective in achieving the valued use, that proponent might well be persuaded to change, refine, exchange the model for the more worthy model. It works better. Demonstration that there is a much better way of achieving the use is a royal road toward changing the model.

The extreme test is whether I would be willing to replace my model with a theory of truth if a theory of truth were better able to help me achieve my valued use. My answer is yes, yes indeed. My goals are so important to me that I would adopt any conceptual system that could help me to become the person that I am capable of becoming, and to be free of the painful scenes in my personal world. I would adopt some other model. I would even adopt a theory of truth. Showing that this other conceptual system is better able to help me attain my goal is a truly persuasive argument for models of usefulness.

Much less so in theories. Theories are indebted to their notions of truth, to their fundamental notions of what is true, what is basic, of the way the world is. Their fundamental truths are not necessarily violated or endangered if some other theory claims it can do a better job in some applied work. Cognitive theory is not going to tremble, or turn itself in for serious modifications, if some other theory claims that its applied interventions manage to get lower scores on measures of depression. You will have to do much more than that to convince a theory that it has to be changed.

What are sufficient grounds for you to abandon the concept or conceptual system?

This is a tough test that models generally pass and theories generally fail. A psychotherapy practitioner, researcher or theorist holds to some favorite concept or hallowed conceptual system. The psychotherapist truly believes in the notion of a self, an irrational cognition, a need for affiliation, in the notion that a patient–therapist relationship is a prerequisite to successful psychotherapy, in the psychoanalytic theory of personality, in social-learning theory, in the law of effect. In fact, the psychotherapist seems to hold to the concept or conceptual system so fervently that I start to wonder if anything could dislodge it. Could there possibly be any reasonably conceivable evidence that the person would honestly accept as sufficient to let go of that preciously clung-to concept or conceptual system? Any at all? All too often, the answer is no.

It seemed sensible to me that just about any concept or entire conceptual system ought to be truly open to some kinds of reasonable grounds that the proponent would accept as declaring the concept or conceptual system to be wrong, false, inadequate, enough to let it go, drop it, abandon it (see Popper, 1972a, 1972b, 1980). A concept or conceptual system 'should, even if true, be held in suspicion and, for purely methodological reasons, in fact be considered erroneous'

(Weinsheimer, 1985, p. 7, see Gadamer, 1975). The test challenges the proponent to spell out the actual grounds that the proponent would accept as sufficient to give up the concept or conceptual system (Mahrer, 1995a, 1996/2004, 1998, 1999).

There are at least three parts to this test. The first is that you specify the concept or the conceptual system that you are willing to put on the block. Suppose it is the concept of the patient–therapist relationship as a prerequisite to successful psychotherapy. Suppose it is the whole system of mental illnesses and disorders. Suppose it is your cognitive–behavioral or psychoanalytic approach. The second is passed when you actually spell out the actual grounds that you would accept as sufficient to give up, abandon, the particular concept or conceptual system. The third is when the grounds are fulfilled, you admit that the grounds are fulfilled, and then you dutifully and honorably give up that hallowed concept or the entire conceptual system.

Remember, the test means that the grounds you specify must be reasonable ones. You are not accepting the spirit of the test, or playing by the rules, if the grounds you specify are not obtainable, could never be sufficient or are otherwise unreasonable, e.g. you may issue a public statement that you would actually abandon your client-centered approach if research could show that this relationship played no role in therapeutic change. However, you refuse to be the one to spell out the research grounds that would be accepted by you as sufficient. Furthermore, it becomes clear that no body of research could ever conclusively convince you that the client-centered relationship played absolutely no role whatsoever in therapeutic change. Finally, it also becomes clear that you cannot even conceive of research that would lead you to conclude that the grounds have been met. Instead of being willing to spell out whatever grounds you would accept, you choose the clever role of being the one to be convinced by whatever grounds someone else might put before you. None of these games is to be used by you. Instead, the grounds are to be reasonable ones and to be set down by you in a spirit of playing the game reasonably, sensibly and honorably.

Theories of truth rarely if ever spell out the kinds of evidence that would be sufficient to drop the theory, to let it go. To do this, the theory would have to say that this kind of research would be sufficient. If this research has these kinds of findings, then I consider those findings sufficient to abandon the theory of truth, e.g. if I hold to a theory

of evolution, would any findings from studying fossil records be sufficient for me to let go of my theory of evolution? If I think along these
lines, I may never even begin doing this kind of research, because
entire sets of negative findings would still be insufficient: 'the theory
of evolution cannot be disproved by any evidence from the fossil
record: the fossil record can only tell us how evolution occurred and
which particular pathways it took, not whether or not theory of evolution is true' (Dunbar, 1995, p. 23).

In psychotherapy, it is almost inconceivable that a cognitive theorist
or a psychoanalytic theorist, or any other proponent of a theory,
would even be willing to try to spell out the grounds that would be
sufficient to abandon the theory. Even if they tried to put sufficient evidence down on the table, it is almost impossible that such research
could produce such findings. The contract must be clear: if I show you
this evidence, then you agree to abandon your theory, right? I have
almost never found such a contract in psychotherapy.

Suppose that we moved over to more logical grounds. Suppose that
you seriously and sincerely accepted the rule that, if a concept made
no significant difference in what you do in actual in-session therapeutic work, the concept is to be dropped, even if it is basic and
foundational. Do you accept the rule? Suppose that you accept the
rule, at least to see what happens if you play the game. Suppose we
start with your hallowed concept of self. What would you do differently in actual therapeutic work if you dropped the notion of self, if
there were no self or if you conceived of multiple selves, with no single overall executive leader self? If you could not come up with
significant differences that would happen in your therapy, if you
would insist on doing pretty much the same thing, if you cannot come
up with substantial things that you would do differently, are you sincerely ready to let go of the notion of self?

In general, theories of truth usually find this test much too tough to
pass. Theories of truth usually fail it. The history of psychotherapeutic theories is simply not full of worthy examples where some theory
actually went to the trouble of spelling out the necessary grounds that
would be reasonable and sufficient for the concept or the theory itself
to be abandoned, went ahead and saw whether the grounds were present, concluded that they were indeed present, and then dutifully
abandoned the concept or the theory itself. Theories simply do not risk
failing such a test. Concepts fade away, lose favor, are even aban-

doned. So too are theories. However, these happen because of all sorts of reasons that have little or nothing to do with the theory submitting itself to this test, failing the test and abdicating the throne in good faith.

Theories often put on a show of saying that they submit themselves to testing. Both researchers and theoreticians pride themselves in saying publicly that they 'test' their theories. Theories proclaim that they are deservedly scientific because so much work goes into continuously testing them. Things can become quite tense if you ask to see the tests of some explicit concept or conceptual system. Once you are handed the actual tests, things can get downright deadly serious or knee-slappingly hilarious if you study all the material that you are given and then say: 'I have not found any instances where so-called "testing" included the laying out of reasonable grounds that would be accepted as sufficient to drop, abandon, let go of the concept or the theory, with perhaps these two exceptions where the concepts were unimportant, lightweight, tertiary concepts that were almost irrelevant in the whole conceptual system.' It seems that testing a truly important concept or a whole theory virtually never means stating and acting honorably on the reasonable grounds that would be deemed sufficient to drop the important concept or the whole theory! If that is the case, it is a deceptive mistake or outright lie to say that the theory submits itself to true testing. It would be more honest to say that theories submit themselves to testing that does not endanger giving up the tested concept or theory. In other words, the important concepts and theories are really not submitted to testing.

The case is offered that theories generally fail to submit themselves to this test: what are the reasonably sufficient grounds for you to abandon that particular important concept or that theory?

If this case holds, and it seems to hold, then theorists join with psychotics and cultists in having deep-seated truths that are held impervious to reasonable evidence that psychotics, cultists and theorists would accept as sufficient to let go of their deep-seated truths. Perhaps a main difference between theorists, on the one hand, and psychotics and cultists, on the other, is that theorists like to proclaim that they are scientific, open to empirical evidence, willing to test their important concepts and theories, and willing to abandon them if they are presented with reasonable evidence. In other words, perhaps the main difference is that psychotics and cultists are more honest than theorists!

In almost stark contrast, models actually welcome this test. Models tend to be sincere when they say: 'Let's try it out. Look at the results of trying it out. If the actual task, job, usefulness calls for some different model, let us drop the present model in favor of the more fitting model that comes from taking a good look at the actual workability and usefulness, at the findings.' Models pride themselves in coming from what seems to work. They pride themselves on being dispensable, useful. Models pride themselves on being useful, not on having to be true. Models have much less invested in being true; they are useful, not true. For models, the ordinary test goes like this: the reasonable grounds for abandoning this particular concept or whole conceptual system is that some other one does a better job of coming from and fitting the actual findings, the actual demonstrated usefulness.

In general, theories rarely if ever face this test, and rarely if ever risk passing or failing this test. In general, models are far more willing to face this test, and to welcome actually passing or failing this test.

Personality parts: universally true or restricted to particular theories or models?

Theories include pieces and bits, components and elements, all sorts of things that are parts of what is called 'personality'. These include such things as egos, conceptual schemata, primary affects, maternal instincts, core cognitions, unconscious impulses, effectance motivations, basic needs and drives, stages of developments, psycho-pathological processes, intrapsychic conflicts, supraordinate cognitions, defense mechanisms, paranoid states, borderline conditions, seasonal affective disorders, attention deficit disorders, proactive inhibitions, abusive personalities and dozens and dozens of other parts and processes and personality components.

The theories that invent these personality parts believe them to be true. Not only are they real and true, but they exist above and beyond the various theories. They are universal. All theories should salute them. If psychoanalytic theory knows that there are egos, then cognitive theory, and all theories, should acknowledge that there are egos. If cognitive theory invented 'cognitive schemata', cognitive theory expects that all theories, including psychoanalytic theory, will salute 'cognitive schemata', because they are universal.

Each theory invents its own personality parts, and then tries hard to raise those personality parts to universal personality parts that all other theories are to accept as universal. The net result is that every theory is to accept that all of these things are universal, theory-free and real: from attention deficit disorders to proactive inhibition, from unconscious impulses to core cognitions, from effectance motivations to the anal stage of psychosexual development.

This takes an almost ugly form when dominant theories use incredible pressure, backroom politics, arm-twisting and power tactics to force all theories to bow down to the dominant theories' personality parts as universal, theory-free. It is to be universally accepted, by every theory and approach, that there are things such as basic needs and drives, egos, core cognitions, stages of psychosexual development, psychopathological processes, mental illnesses and diseases, etc.

Models do not believe in the truth of these personality parts. Models believe that all of these personality parts are invented by particular theories and are restricted to the particular theories that invented them. None of these things is either real and true or universal and theory-free. Particular theories invented unconscious impulses or core cognitions, and these and other such things are restricted to the theories that invented them in the first place. This is the position that models hold.

Incompatible rivals or friendly alternatives?

Theories are almost ordained to be in an everlasting war with other theories because each theory proclaims that it knows what is really true, that there is only one grand truth and that there can be only one best approximation of that one truth. Accordingly, all other theories are likely to be rivals, in opposition, enemies. Their basic beliefs about truth, beliefs they almost all share, practically insure that theories are incompatible rivals over the truth, e.g. there has been a long-standing war between rival theories of truth over whether or not the external world is real, true, veridical. Some theories of truth proclaim that the external world is indeed real. There is an external reality. In stark opposition are other theories of truth that just as stoutly proclaim that there is no real external world. People invent, fabricate, build, construct their own personal worlds that are unreal, illusory. As both camps are theories of truths, only one can be true. If one is true, then the other camp must be less true or untrue. They have a long history of war-like rivalry with one another.

Most of the people in science, and most of the people in religion, share a mind-set of theories of truth. This almost certainly means that they will find deep and serious issues on which they fundamentally differ and are in incompatible opposition (e.g. Haught, 1995). How did the world begin? What is the ultimate explanation of human life, inexplicable catastrophes, ultimate faith, unexplainable deaths? According to the rules of the mind-set, if science is right, religion is wrong; if religion is closer to the truth, science must be further from the truth. Science and religion must regard each other as incompatible rivals on issues that they both regard as their subject matter, when they both share a mind-set of theories of truth. It is a war, a serious contest for who wins and who loses.

Models watch from the sidelines. They are inclined to see that battle as limited to theories of truth, and as an irrelevant, groundless, non-issue for models (Mahrer, 1995b), e.g. in the experiential model (Mahrer, 1989, 1995b, 1996/2004) a person is pictured as having a number of ways of creating, building, designing his or her own personal world, which may be real or unreal, by using building blocks that may qualify as exceedingly real or exceedingly unreal. This experiential model is entertained mainly because it is useful in helping to do the jobs for which the experiential model was created. If some other model is more useful, it would probably be adopted.

Models tend to be friendly toward other models created for the same or for different purposes; theories tend to regard other theories as incompatible rivals for the single supreme truth. 'To propose something as a *model* of [an] x is to suggest it as a way of representing x ... ; moreover, it is to admit the possibility of alternative representations useful of different purposes. To propose something as a *theory* of [an] x, on the other hand, is to suggest that x's *are* governed by such and such principles. Accordingly, the scientist who proposes something as a theory of [an] x must hold that alternative theories are to be rejected, or modified, or understood as holding only for special cases, or something of the like' (Achinstein, 1965, p. 105). If the x refers to a phenomenon such as dreaming or suddenly becoming scared when you are talking with another person, two theories will be inclined to view one another as rivals. One must be superior – that is the way it is for theories of truth. On the other hand, models believe that alternative or even irreconcilable models can both be good, worthwhile, applicable when applied to the same x, to the same phenomenon. Physicists who use models know this: 'If we restrict ourselves to invoking considerations of pure logic, we cannot prevent a physicist from representing different sets of laws, or even a single group of laws, by several irreconcilable theories' (Duhem, 1996, p. 66).

In theories of truth, two different and opposing theories of the same phenomenon are almost certainly at war. Both cannot be correct. In models of usefulness, two different and opposing models may well both be of worth, intact, useful. This difference between theories and models is shown in the difference between what is referred to as French theories of geometry and English models of physics.

> For a geometer of the school of Laplace and Couchy, it would be absurd to give two distinct explanations of one law and to maintain that these two explanations are true at the same time. For an English physicist, there is no contradiction in one law being represented in two different ways by two different models.
>
> Duhem (1996, p. 62)

In psychotherapy, the rules for theories of truth hold that two different theories of the same phenomenon almost certainly must vie for which is closer to the truth; models can easily live comfortably with different models of the same phenomenon.

When a model talks with a theory of truth, the model can reassure the theory that the theory can be safe. The model can say, 'You do not have to think of me as a rival. You make pronouncements of truth. I am not a pronouncement of truth. You need not see me as a competitor, because I am not a competitor. So relax. Nor do I see you as a rival. I try to be useful for some particular purpose, and, if you are more useful for that purpose, I cheerfully give way to you as more useful. What this means is that you and I can talk because you need not regard me as a rival, nor do I have a basis for regarding you as a rival.'

Creation of grand alternatives or a single, unified, grand theory?

Both Feyerabend (1972, 1978) and Popper (1972a, 1972b, 1980) encouraged attempts to create bold alternatives to established, accepted, conceptual systems. With a healthy glow of playful enthusiasm, they deliberately carve out grand alternative conceptual systems. Do not close off the field by a kind of benumbed clinging to the traditional, established, accepted conceptual system.

In an important way, models are the conceptual system of choice for this. After all, who knows what better or greater uses may be discovered if one is intentionally open to the creation of bold new models, grand alternative models? Models can be highly appropriate launching pads for the invention of grand alternatives.

Theories are not appropriate, or at least much less so. They tend to be much more conservative. After all, theories must be true. Even the mere intent to look for a grand alternative can be an embarrassing or risky admission that what is generally accepted as true may not really be true. When theories dare to dream, they generally prefer to dream about a single, grand, unified, universal theory of truth. This is part of the wish or hope fuelling the integrative–eclectic movement in psychotherapy.

When theories dare to dream, they dream about being the elevated, lofty, grand theory of everything psychological, the mother of all theories. There is a logic and an order to the psychological world. Each theory can dare to dream about being that grand theory because theories know that there is a single grand truth to nature, to the world of psychological things. Maybe my theory is the grand answer.

When theories dare to dream, they dream about having the answer to everything, of being able to get at the fundamental underlying truth that answers everything, the core truth behind all core truths, the essence of everything psychological. Theories believe that there is such a foundational core truth, and theories can be excused for dreaming of having that answer.

Models have no basis for such grand quests, for such grand and glorious dreams. One reason is that models do not think in terms of truths, whether they are the essential, underlying grand truth or whether they are the single, grand, elevated theory of everything. The other reason is that models are busy carving out or being ready to welcome grand alternatives.

In general, these considerations seem to support a case that models are more open than theories of truth to improvement, modification, advancement and wholesale change or replacement. If you accept this case, then here is another preferential feature of models of usefulness compared with theories of truth.

Foundational truths or basic issues and questions

Theories of truth revolve around what may be called 'foundational truths' such as the following:

1. The brain is a basic determinant of human behavior.
2. There are biopsychological stages of human development.
3. Scientific research is to confirm or disconfirm testable hypotheses.

These foundational truths underlie psychotherapy theory, research, practice, education–training. Later I provide a list of many of these foundational truths.

These foundational truths are the cornerstones on which theories of truth rest. They are the basic principles, the fundamental starting points, what is taken as the rock-bottom givens or basic truths. 'Foundational truths' are in the spirit of what has been referred to as theorems, postulates, axioms, canons, dictums, self-evident truths. They are the core of theories of truth. Some foundational truths are so basic that they are beyond research confirmation and disconfirmation. Some foundational truths may be shown to need modification on the basis of cumulative research. The precise wording may be improved, modified, refined. Over the course of time, some foundational truths may be inclined to fade away or be replaced by other foundational truths. Yet at the very core of theories of truth are foundational truths.

Not so in models of usefulness. Models revolve around basic issues and basic questions. Models come into being as positions on basic issues or answers to basic questions. Models respect and honor basic issues and basic questions. If you think in terms of theories of truths, your core consists of foundational truths. If you think in terms of models of usefulness, your core consists of basic issues and questions.

Basic issues and questions are two sides of the same coin, i.e. the proposition may be stated as a basic issue or a basic question. In what follows, the form will be that of basic questions rather that basic issues, but it may be stated either way.

Why do theories of truth have so much less respect for basic issues and questions?

Basic issues and questions have the utmost respect from models of usefulness. In stark contrast, they have very little respect from theories of truth. There are some reasons for this:

- Theories rely on foundational truths. When you already rely on a series of foundational truths, there is very little room for relying on a series of basic issues and questions. You already have your core, your anchoring foundation.

- Theories of truth would not especially like the idea that their foundational truths are not really foundational, that there are basic issues and questions that underlie foundational truths, that their precious foundational truths are really little more than a position on some more basic issue or just one answer to some more basic question, e.g. the foundational truth 'the brain is a basic determinant of human behavior' is merely one answer to the more basic question 'What are the determinants of human behavior?'. The foundational truth 'scientific research is to confirm or disconfirm testable hypotheses' may be merely one answer to the more fundamental, underlying, basic question 'What are the aims and purposes of doing research?'

- Theories of truth would probably tend to see basic issues and questions as grist for the research mill. Instead of being a basic question, theories of truth would be inclined to see them as a research question. If a basic question has been around for centuries, theories are entitled to say: 'We now have the research designs and tools to answer that empirical question.' Give yourself a test. When you read the basic questions in the next section, see how easy it is to adopt a mind-set that many of them are merely 'empirical questions', answerable by research.

- Theories of truth can be understood as looking at a series of basic questions and saying: 'But we have answered those question! We have the answers. Here are the research-based answers.' And then the theory proceeds to say what the answers are. In contrast, models are inclined to see these as almost eternal basic questions, if they are worded well. The field can provide an answer, but providing an answer does not mean that the basic question goes away. There can be multiple answers to the same basic question, and there can be better and better answers in the future – so say the models of usefulness.

Models of usefulness have the utmost respect for basic questions. Theories of truth have little or no respect for basic questions, and there seem to be some reasons for this.

Examples of 'basic questions'

Models honor and respect basic issues and questions. They treasure such a valued list. Theories much prefer their 'foundational truths'. Theories have little or no reason to identify a list of basic issues and questions. The following is an illustrative sampling of some basic questions that are so central to most models. The list is organized under four topics: conceptualization, research, personality, and psychotherapy and personal change.

Conceptualization

- Under what conditions can one conceptual system encompass and incorporate another conceptual system?
- Can constructs in one conceptual system relate to and have effects on constructs in a different conceptual system?
- Are biological, neurological and chemical events and variables basic to psychological events and variables?
- Is the psychological world lawful and organized, or not especially so?
- Are there psychological laws of human nature? If so, what are they?
- What accounts for the foundational beliefs of a given psychological theorist, researcher, practitioner or teacher–trainer?
- What accounts for foundational beliefs being hidden, concealed, unknown?
- How can conceptual systems be improved, advanced?
- What are the 'breakthrough problems' in regard to conceptual systems?
- What are the sensible and reasonable grounds for abandoning a given conceptual system?
- How can a conceptual system be constructed, originated, generated?
- How can a conceptual system be judged as superior to and better than rival conceptual systems?
- Can a conceptual system provide an approximation of what is true?
- On what basis may a conceptual system be judged as adequate or inadequate?
- How can one determine the truth or falsity of a conceptual statement?
- What psychotherapeutic data are trusted as hard, objective and real?
- What are the criteria for judging psychotherapeutic data as hard, objective and real?
- If a measure is precise and real, does that mean that what it measures is precise and real?
- What constitutes the hard, real, objective evidence for the meaning of a conceptual term or construct?
- On what basis can conceptual phrases and terms such as 'mental illness'

or 'psychopathology' be judged as real or as unreal creations of a given conceptual system?
- What are the criteria for determining how something works and operates?
- How can 'causes' be distinguished from 'accompanying and correlative events'?
- Does a person relate to a phenomenon as fearful and threatening because a person relates to it in fear and threat?
- What are the criteria for determining that one causal explanation is superior to its plausible rivals?
- What accounts for a conceptual system gaining wider general acceptance than its rivals?
- What is the relationship between 'folk psychologies' and 'designated conceptual systems' in psychotherapy?
- On what basis does a given psychotherapeutic theorist, researcher or practitioner accept or reject an alien conceptual system?
- What determines the 'threat value' of an alien conceptual system?
- To what extent do 'standard' terms and phrases contain or not contain implicit and concealed conceptual baggage?

Research

- To what extent and in what ways does a psychotherapy researcher's belief system determine what to study, how to study it and what can be found?
- Do standard and accepted research designs and methods lead to, limit and truncate the research questions, or do the research questions lead to, determine and originate the research design and methods?
- What are the determinants of the degree to which a researcher can know and set aside the researcher's own belief system?
- Which position is more powerful, pertinent and useful: (1) a researcher's findings determine the researcher's belief system or (2) a researcher's belief system determines the researcher's findings?
- What accounts for a piece of knowledge being put into or taken out of the cumulative body of psychotherapeutic knowledge?
- What are the useful and effective means and avenues of increasing psychotherapeutic knowledge?
- Has psychotherapy accumulated a large degree of the knowledge that can be known, or has it barely scratched the surface?
- Has psychotherapeutic knowledge come largely from research, clinical practice or some other resource?
- Is there one 'scientific method' or are there several different kinds of 'scientific methods'?
- How can research be done to show that a hypothesis is false, refuted and shown to be wrong?
- What are precise and rigorous methods of arriving at a research hypothesis?

- How can research be designed to have a rigorous effect on the conceptual system from which the hypothesis is generated?
- Why do researchers do research on psychotherapy? What are the various aims, purposes and goals of doing research on psychotherapy?
- What are the criteria for the worth and importance of a research project?
- What are the relationships between research findings and psychotherapeutic practice?

Personality

- Where does personality come from in the first place? Where does it all begin?
- What are the pieces and bits, the components and parts, of what is referred to as 'personality'?
- What accounts for behavior, behavior development and change?
- How and why does a person have feelings that are good and pleasant, or bad and unpleasant?
- How and why does a person build, construct, organize his or her own personal world?
- What accounts for the relationship between the person and the external world?
- How do social phenomena come about?
- What accounts for ordinary and common personality change?
- What accounts for personality change that is deep-seated, transformational or radical?
- What determines the limits and the scope of personality change over the course of a life?
- What determines the kind of person that the person can become?

Psychotherapy and personal change

- What are the purposes, aims and goals of psychotherapy and personal change?
- How can a person identify the aims and goals of psychotherapy for the other person?
- On what basis is an identified aim or goal judged as superior to or better than other plausible aims and goals for this given person?
- What are the determinants of a change in the aims and purposes of psychotherapy with this given person?
- What determines whether the aims and goals of psychotherapy emphasize a reduction of the problematic and upholding the 'normal', or achieving the optimal and the possible?
- What are the defining characteristics of what is understood as psychotherapy?

- How can different schools of, or approaches to, psychotherapy be identified and distinguished from one another?
- What are the foundational beliefs and underlying principles of psychotherapy as differentiated from related enterprises?
- What accounts for clients and psychotherapists seeking each other out and having conversations with each another?
- What kinds of information are especially useful in determining which methods are to be used?
- What determines whether past events are to be useful, which past events are useful and how past events are useful?
- Who predominantly carries out the methods of change: the psychotherapist or the person?
- What methods are useful in enabling the person to undergo a radical, qualitative and transformational personal change?
- What are the most useful and effective ways for therapists and clients to be with one another?
- How does the therapist gain meaning from what a person is saying and doing?
- How can a therapist know what the other person is feeling, thinking, undergoing and experiencing?

See the difference?

If theories of truth rely on their foundational truths and models of usefulness instead rely on their 'basic issues' or 'basic questions', what do the differences actually look like? How might the differences actually show themselves?

To see the differences, I give some foundational truths that are relatively common to many theorists of truth in the field of psychotherapy. Of course, you may take exception to the 'foundational truths'. You may want to refine or modify the actual wording. Or you may doubt that these are indeed 'foundational truths' that are accepted by a fair number of theories. You may be right.

However, if you can allow for the possibility that these may illustrate some relatively common foundational truths, each is followed by what a particular model, an experiential model (Mahrer, 1989) has to say is its alternative. In each pair, the foundational truth is given first, and what follows is the experiential model's position on the underlying basic issue or answer to the underlying basic question. In other words, in each of the following pairs, the first answers the question 'What is a relatively common "foundational truth"?' and the second answers the question 'What is one model's alternative?'

1. There is a cumulative body of psychotherapeutic knowledge; research is a primary gatekeeper for what is admitted into or withdrawn out of the cumulative body of knowledge.

   Each distinctive conceptual approach has its own relatively distinctive body of knowledge; research plays a minor role in what is admitted into or withdrawn out of each conceptual approach's body of knowledge.

2. Prediction and explanation of empirically validated facts are important criteria for judging the worth of theories of psychotherapy.

   Conceptual systems of psychotherapy are to be judged largely on the basis of their demonstrated usefulness in helping to achieve the aims for which the conceptual systems were generated and used.

3. Theories of psychotherapy are judged, examined and tested by deriving hypotheses that are subjected to scientific verification, confirmation, disconfirmation, refutation and falsification.

   Conceptual systems as models of usefulness, rather than theories of truth, are to be revised, improved or replaced largely on the basis of their demonstrated usefulness, lack of usefulness or comparative usefulness relative to plausible alternative models.

4. Biological, neurological, physiological and chemical events and variables are basic to psychological events and variables.

   In the philosophy of science accepted by the experiential model, the events that are of interest are described and understood in terms of the experiential system of constructs, rather than in terms of supposedly more basic events and variables in such bodies of constructs as biology, neurology, physiology and chemistry.

5. Human beings have inborn, intrinsic biological and psychological needs, drives, instincts and motivations; these include needs and drives for survival, sex, aggression, object-seeking and contact comfort.

   Each person is understood in terms of deeper and basic 'potentials for experiencing' that are relatively unique to this person, rather than universal, experiential, rather than biological or biopsychological, and not characterized by properties of need, drive or force.

6. There are biopsychological stages of human growth and development.

   A person's initially established system of potentials and their relationships is ordinarily continued throughout life, rather than being established by, and subsequent changes occurring as a consequence of, what many perspectives accept as biological stages of human growth and development.

7. Responses followed by satisfying consequences tend to be strengthened; responses followed by unsatisfying consequences tend to be weakened.

   Behavior tends to be adopted and maintained depending, in large part, on its effectiveness in building the kind of personal world that it is important for the person to have, and its effectiveness in enabling the kind of experiencing that it is important for the person to undergo.

8. There are mental illnesses, diseases or disorders.

The experiential model has no place, use or meaning for the non-experiential notion, idea, concept or construct of mental illnesses, diseases or disorders.

9. Clients seek psychotherapy for, and psychotherapy is, treatment of psychological–psychiatric problems, distresses, mental disorders, personal difficulties and problems in living.

Clients seek psychotherapy as a situational context for the experience of potentials for experiencing and their relationships.

10. The practitioner initially assesses and diagnoses the problem or mental disorder, and then selects and applies the appropriate treatment.

In each experiential session, including the initial session, the person starts by finding a scene of strong feeling, and then proceeds through in-session steps toward becoming the qualitatively new person that he or she is capable of becoming, and to be free of the initial painful scene-situation.

11. The proper therapist–client relationship is a prerequisite to successful psychotherapy.

The therapist and the client predominantly attending to one another constitutes a helpful condition for both participants undergoing feelings and experiences that are personally important for each to undergo in the session.

In general, the case is that theories of truth tend to rely on a base of foundational truths, whereas models of usefulness are inclined to rely on positions on basic issues or answers to basic questions. Each has its own mind-set and each can probably make a case on behalf of its own advantages and strengths.

A way of resolving some of the unresolved problems of theories of truth

Theories of truth have a way of creating some deep, serious problems that are seemingly unresolvable. Many of these problems have defied solution for centuries. Theories of truth bring about these problems for themselves by assuming that the entities they create are real and true. Here are a few examples:

- What are the relationships between mind and body?
- Is there something referred to as schizophrenia or is schizophrenia a non-existent myth?
- Does God exist or is God another non-existent myth?

Theories of truth tend to create these ancient tough problems by assuming that both alternatives must somehow be true, i.e. it must be true that either there are or there are not minds and bodies. If they exist, the secondary problem is how they relate to one another. It must be true that either there is or there is not something referred to as 'schizophrenia'. It must be true that God either exists or does not exist. If you believe that God exists, you are almost forced to believe that God is the creator, and evolution is not a plausible alternative.

In general, theories of truth bring on themselves these kinds of virtually unresolvable problems, and proponents of theories of truth can and will argue for centuries largely because each side holds the truth of its beliefs. Indeed, there is essentially no way out, little or no chance for resolution.

Models offer a solution that is acceptable to proponents of models, but not especially acceptable to the warring sides who both believe in the truthfulness of what they hold as true. Models can accept that some things are concrete, real, true. Models can also hold that many other things are convenient fictions, useful entities to create, but not real or true. For models, convenient fictions can include mind, body, schizophrenia, God and many other things. If they are convenient fictions, the problem can be resolved in at least two ways. One way is that a proponent of a model can accept the convenient fiction that there is or is not a mind, with the choice depending on which convenient fiction is more useful for some use, some goal or aim. If God is a convenient fiction, the proponent of a model can use that convenient fiction if it is useful. One can or cannot use the convenient fiction of schizophrenia, depending on the intended use. A second way of resolving the problem is that many secondary problems become illusory when both sides consist of convenient fictions. For theories of truth, the relationship between mind and body is a serious problem. Whether God is the ultimate creator or there is a plausible alternative becomes a serious problem for theories of truth. But these secondary problems wash away as illusory for proponents of models of usefulness. If mind and body are convenient fictions, there is no problem of how they relate to each other as if there really are minds and bodies that must somehow relate to one another.

Theories of truth create some tough, unresolved problems. Models of usefulness offer a way of solving those problems, but the solution is virtually unavailable to those whose mind-sets are locked into theories of truth.

What options are available when there is a clash?

Picture opposing views on a controversial issue. Here is one of many examples from psychotherapy: 'What mainly accounts for therapeutic change?' One relatively strong camp holds that the therapist–client relationship mainly accounts for therapeutic change. An opposing camp holds that the use of effective techniques, effective interventions, mainly accounts for therapeutic change. How can the matter be resolved? What kinds of options are sensibly available?

If your mind-set is one of theories of truth, you will be inclined toward at least the following ways of resolving the matter:

- One defeats the other. One is closer to the truth and it will probably win out when enough of the right kind of research and clear thinking are done.
- The answer might include an integration of the two. Both sides are true, in their own ways. You can get closer to the truth by combining both. The question is how to integrate the two sides in the best way that comes closer to the truth.

If your mind-set is one of models of usefulness, you also will probably have a number of additional options for resolving the controversy:

- The answer varies with, and depends on, the intended use. For this particular use, it may be most convenient to rely on the therapist–client relationship; for that particular use, the answer might be to rely on the right interventions; for a third given use, the answer may be to combine the two in this or that way.

If you think in terms of models of usefulness, you may be drawn toward two other options for resolving the controversy:

- The controversial issue may be resolved by learning more about the conceptual systems or models, i.e. one conceptual system or model would probably incline the user to believe that the answer lies in the therapist–client relationship, and other conceptual systems or models would incline the user to favor therapist methods and interventions, or some combination of both. In other words, when there is a clash between two sides on a controversial issue, the task is not to see which one is more right. Rather the opportunity is to appreciate how the different conceptual systems or models differ from one another.

- What underlying presumption do the two opposing views share in common, and what is a grand third alternative? For there to be a controversy, the two sides would almost certainly share a common underlying notion or idea, e.g. both sides may well presume that, in psychotherapy, whether there is a therapist–client relationship or the therapist is using various techniques, the therapist and the client are attending mainly to one another. If this is a common underlying presumption, what might be some other underlying presumption that offers a grand third alternative? Suppose that you think of therapeutic change as from neither the therapist–client relationship nor the therapist's bag of therapeutic methods and techniques, both of which presume that therapist and client are attending mainly to one another. Suppose that the grand alternative is that therapeutic change comes from things that can be done when both the therapist and the client are attending mainly to an important third focal center of attention, rather than mainly to one another.

It seems that a mind-set of theories of truth and a mind-set of models of usefulness are inclined toward favoring different ways of doing something about a clash between two sides on some controversial issue.

Useful pictures over easy conceptual explanations?

When theories look at some event, some phenomenon, some change, theories know that perhaps the highest-level, most revered, most stringent questions they can ask are: 'How can we explain that?', 'What is the explanation of that?', 'Why did that occur?' These are the truly important questions when theories face something called dreams, or special kinds of dreams such as nightmares or dreams that foretell significant future events or dreams where the dreamer can direct what will happen. These are the truly important questions when theories face a person who is severely depressed or unaccountably leaves her solid Midwest family and goes to live on a Greek island, a person who suddenly tries to suffocate his father-in-law, an average child who grows up to become the most famous actor in the world, the ordinary fellow who suddenly seems to go berserk, the young girl who speaks with the voice of God.

Theories love to ask these questions and to provide the very best conceptual explanations. Indeed, most theories elevate the provision of the very best possible explanation to the highest plateau of what theories do. Scientific theorizing includes offering the truest possible conceptual explanation. Theories are judged on their ability to approximate the true conceptual explanation. A fine theory prides itself on valuing and providing the true conceptual explanation. They vie with one another. The theory that provides the truest conceptual explanation is saluted by its rivals, revered and disliked by its rivals. A theory that is unable to provide a fine conceptual explanation is almost no theory at all, and can be ridiculed by bigger and better theories.

Models barely bother. They know they can produce loads of conceptual explanations with all the ease of a popcorn popper. Production of conceptual explanations is for kids who play, not for serious work. It can be fun to produce a whole bunch of conceptual explanations, and it is so easy. However, models have more serious work to do. Models get serious in creating useful pictorializations, rather than participating in the playful game of producing conceptual explanations. Models generally decline to play that game, and much prefer generating pictures that are workable, that are useful (Apostel, 1961). Let us be clear. As far as models are concerned, conceptual explanations are lightweight, easy, cheap and don't add up to much when it comes to actual usefulness.

Challenging the usefulness of theoretical explanations

When it comes to sheer, practical, on-the-job usefulness, models are quite skeptical about how thoroughgoing theoretical explanations stack up. Indeed, models take a rather tough stance on which theoretical explanations are comparatively second-rate with regard to down-to-earth usefulness.

Theories generally accept the idea that, if the theoretical explanation is fine, true, the theoretical explanation should, of course, offer sure-fire, helpful leads or cues to attaining the goal or use that you have in mind. Explain the phenomenon well, and you should be able to accomplish what you want with or about the phenomenon. If the person is seriously depressed, trust the best theoretical explanation of depression. Is the best explanation one of inadequate cognitions, or one in which the depression is a symptom of a mental disease or disorder, or one involving repressed aggressive impulses turned upon oneself? One explanation may be the best, the truest, the most rigorously tested. The truest guideline is that, once we know the explanation of depression in this person, we will have trustworthy hints or cues about what can be done to treat the depression, to reduce its severity, to do something helpful and even useful with the depression.

Theories generally start with the thing to be explained, e.g. the depression, and then get hints for how to treat the depression from the theory's explanation of what depression is. Models generally go in the opposite direction. Models think like this: there can be lots and lots of explanations of a supposedly fixed entity called 'depression'. We prefer to start with the use, the aim, the intent and then find the most useful picture (not explanation) for purposes of that use, aim, intent, e.g. in the experiential model, the intent is generally to discover what underlies the experience of this depression, what is deeper, the 'deeper potential for experience' that this person can become. In addition, if this experience of depression is painful, the additional use is for the person to be free of this painful depression and the painful scenes in which it occurs. The point is that the experiential model has whatever picture of depression is most useful for the intended uses. The picture is not of an isolated, continuing, subject entity called 'depression'. Instead, the picture is of depression as useful for the intended uses.

When the aim is to attain some use, then models challenge theories: 'For this or that designated use, our picture of the thing, e.g. depression, is more useful than your explanation of what you call depression.'

There is a related reason why models confidently challenge the usefulness of theories' explanations. Whatever models conceive of, invent, postulate, make up, models do so largely because it is useful to conceive of, construct or construe the thing in that way, e.g. for models the question of 'personality' goes like this: 'What is the most useful way of thinking of, conceiving of, picturing "personality" for the particular uses we have in mind?' In the experiential model, one use is for the person to become the qualitatively whole new person that he or she is capable of becoming, and the coupled other use is for the person to be free of his or her painful scenes and the painful feeling in those scenes. With these uses in mind, a model of personality is conceived, invented, constructed, pictorialized. This model simply includes potentials for experiencing in relationship to one another. This conceptualization of personality is generated because it is the most useful for our two uses or aims. It is not generated because it is supposedly true, because that is what personality is really like. Accordingly, personality is naïvely free of such things as intrapsychic dynamics, egos, core cognitions, psychobiological needs and drives, traits, metacognitions, effectance motivations, psychopathological processes, defenses, etc.

It is likely that most theories do not portray personality simply in terms of potentials for experiencing in relationship to one another. Most theories would probably not even conceive of potentials for experiencing in relationship with one another because theories do not generate their conceptualizations of personality by starting with their valued and intended uses. Instead, theories almost uniformly start with the firm belief that there really and truly are things that comprise personality. There really and truly are, depending on the theory, such things as egos, unconscious impulses, core cognitions, metacognitions, needs and drives, traits, intrapsychic psychodynamics, pathological processes, etc.

As models' pictures of personality come from the most useful pictures for the designated uses, and as theories' explanations of personality come from a notion of what personality is really and truly like, it seems likely that models' pictures of personality are far more useful than theories' explanations of personality.

There is a third reason why models are so ready to challenge the comparative usefulness of theoretical explanations. Most theories have a limited set of uses of whatever thing, phenomenon or event that the theory explains. It is rather likely that the limited set of uses does not include that designated use that the model has directly in mind, e.g. suppose that a theory has its best explanation for a particular person's deeper quality of defiance and rebelliousness. Given the explanation, what are the implied, built-in, likely uses of having explained the deeper quality? One built-in use may be to have insight and understanding of the deeper defiance and rebelliousness. Another built-in use may be to strengthen defenses against that deeper defiance and rebelliousness. Perhaps a third use is for the person to be vigilant toward and to guard against the outbreak of the deeper defiance and rebelliousness. Whatever the range of built-in uses, it is not necessarily true that the uses will include the model's main valued use of becoming a qualitatively whole new person, with the deeper quality of defiance and rebelliousness becoming an integral part of the whole new person.

Each of these considerations points toward the same conclusion: compared with models' pictorializations of some thing, phenomenon or event, theoretical explanations are weaker when it comes to some designated use, aim, intent or goal. In general, models seem to have good reasons for challenging the comparative usefulness of theoretical explanations. Models can entertain the idea that most theoretical explanations are relatively useless.

Explanation: the serious work of serious science or a simple, playful game?

If a theory does what a fine theory has to do, the theory will provide a serious explanation. This person clearly seems to be conspicuously different from the way the person has consistently been up to now. A qualitative shift has occurred. The theory's job includes the provision of a superior explanation. If the theory is scientific, it provides the superior explanation. Show the theory an event, a phenomenon, and the theory cranks out a scientific explanation. This cranking out of the explanation is to meet the highest standards of logic, careful reasoning. Deduction is to be done rigorously. Induction is to be done rigorously. The explanation itself is to conform to the highest standards of logic. It is to be organized, with internal and external consistency. The explanation is to deal with the reasonable conditions under which the phenomenon occurs. The explanation is to present itself in a way that can be confirmed or refuted, tested and examined.

A fine explanation has to work closely with research. Research provides the empirical facts that the explanation is to explain. New research findings are to be fed into the explanation to see how well the explanation does with the new findings. The explanation produces hypotheses that are tested by research. Several rival explanations compete against one another in contests run by researchers. In so many ways, theories are here to provide fine explanations. That is their job.

Models think of explanations as simple and easy to produce, and as a kind of fun game. However, models have little respect for producing explanations. One reason is that models live in a world in which virtually any phenomenon is quite open to explanation from lots of different perspectives – that conspicuous change in the person is open to a number of different theological explanations, a bunch of different sociological explanations, physiological explanations, chemical explanations, neurological explanations, cultural explanations, a social-learning explanation, a psychoanalytic explanation, a cognitive explanation, an explanation that is Jungian, Adlerian, Sullivanian, etc. etc.

From the perspective of models, any theory worth its salt can provide a solid justification for its explanation (see Taylor, 1973). Precious few theories hang their heads and confess that they are unable to defend their explanations. Models have trouble respecting explanations when just about any explanation can defend itself with a team of defenders.

Models do not believe in some grand single truth that all explanations can reach, i.e. to be the prize for some presumably best explanation (see Feyerabend, 1972). Once the grand single truth is gone, it is hard to show that one explanation comes closer than other explanations to approximating the non-existent grand single truth.

Models do live in a world in which the value lies in achieving the valued use. When theories produce their explanations, models say: 'All those explanations are fine and dandy, but now show me that you can obtain this particular use. Show me what you can do with that great explanation. If the explanation cannot help me to attain that use, then the explanation is useless.'

There may have been a time when both models and theories tried to produce explanations. However, the more that models became clear about their own identities, about what models were and what they can and cannot do, the more models turned their backs on explanation: 'if there is any genuine explanatory function, it has gradually been shifted from the model to the fundamental theory' (Groenewold, 1961, p. 103). All in all, models are inclined to think of explanation provision as simple game playing, but not part of the serious work of scientific attainment of the designated use. Theories worship explanations as the true indication of a truly scientific theory.

Theories camouflage and justify therapist games; models spotlight in-session uses

Picture a therapist who has special, important feelings when he fondles the attractive patient, when the patient reveals secrets to her that the patient has never told anyone, when the patient says that he will do what the therapist knows is best and move away from his wife and children, when the patient agrees that he will start having three sessions a week, when the patient shows that she trusts her therapist by taking off her clothes, when the patient talks over these personal matters only with the therapist and no longer with his wife or best friend or the grandfather who raised him from when he was a child.

Now picture that the therapist is explaining what he or she did in the session, and is doing so in a case discussion, a courtroom, a publication, a report or talking with a colleague or a supervisor. When the therapist thinks in terms of theories, it is not especially difficult for the therapist to use the theory as a suitable justification for what the therapist did in the session. The theory can easily lend itself as an effective camouflage, a good-enough justification. The theory provides plenty of notions, ideas and reasons to account for what the therapist did. The theory offers an acceptable and easily available excuse, especially to others who salute the theory. In this important sense, theories can be thought of as ready excuses for what the therapist might otherwise have a hard time accounting for. If only for this purpose alone, theories can be valuable.

Models are not so well outfitted to serve as justification for what therapists do, do not especially relish having out in the open, and seek justification for doing. Perhaps one of the main reasons is that models put the spotlight of emphasis on the actual uses. Instead of hiding what the therapist may actually do in the session, the model comes into play when the therapist defines the actual use, and can turn to the model as a helpful way of picturing things to do to accomplish that use. It is not especially likely that the therapist would openly acknowledge that he wants the patient to take off her clothes, and the model can provide ways and means of getting the patient to do so. When models are used, the spotlight is more on the actual use, and far less on provision of a justifying excuse for what the therapist is seeking an excuse for.

When models are in a playful mood, and want to tweak theories, models accuse theories of being used without knowing that they are being used. Models tell theories that theories are important only because they justify what the theory user wants to do, carry out, accomplish, e.g. if the therapist wants to have the attractive patient take off her clothes, the therapist will use whatever theory can provide the acceptable excuse for having her take off her clothes. The real worth of a theory does not lie in its truths about the nature of the therapeutic relationship, needs to trust or roots of psychopathology. The real roots of a theory lie in the acts that are carried out using the theory as a justification, in the ways the theory is used. Models wag their finger at the theory and say: 'You are just an excuse for the therapist to get the attractive patient to take off her clothes!' Models do not look at the truths that the theories claim are true. Instead, models look at the acts, consequences, uses from calling on the theories. Theories are grand justifications for closing a school, bombing a village, putting a person in a mental asylum or getting the attractive patient to take off her clothes.

Models are created to enable the person to achieve this or that particular use. Theories are easily created to serve as camouflaging justification for some hidden, covert particular use that the therapist wants to achieve but wants to hide under some cloaking theory.

Rival explanations of theories versus friendliness of models toward each other's pictorializations

Theories tend to compete with each other's explanations because theories have a mind-set in which there is a single grand truth, and the superior theory is the one that comes closest to the truly correct one. Theories, therefore, compete to provide the real and true explanation of why this woman suddenly went berserk and shot so many people in the bar, how schizophrenia comes about, why this fellow became so depressed, why this woman has such trouble giving up her drinking, why this boy has voices inside his head.

When there are several explanations, and each claims to be the psychoanalytic one, a way has to be found to see which competing explanation wins and can present itself as the true psychoanalytic explanation. When there are psychoanalytic, biopsychological, object relations, social learning, cognitive–behavioral and behavioral explanations of how schizophrenia comes about, the rivals know that there must be a winner and losers. One explanation may be crowned, or perhaps a new rival is born of pieces and parts of a number of rival explanations.

Most theories have hired guns who do research to show that their explanation can defeat rival explanations. Researchers put on contests to see who wins. Proponents write essays in favor of one explanation over others. Well-endowed explanations have resources to elevate their own explanation over those of rivals. If there are several explanations, the host theories compete with one another to become the accepted explanation, the best and truest explanation. It is a way to keep plenty of people employed and busy.

Models do not concern themselves with explanations of how schizophrenia comes about, why this person started drinking so heavily, why this person has voices, why this person became so depressed. They concern themselves with pictures that are useful for a defined use. If several pictures claim to be useful for precisely the same use, it is usually easy for users to recognize which picture is more useful, and to use that picture. The simple ease of seeing which picture is more useful helps makes the adoption friendly.

When models focus so exclusively on use, it is easy to see that our models are for similar or different uses. My model is useful in helping me to discover the qualitatively whole new person I can become. Your model is useful for speed in solving intellectual games, enhancing recognition of words on a page or increasing the likelihood of subjects carrying out homework assignments. When our models are for different uses, we can be friendly toward each other's pictorializations. When our models are for essentially the same use, we can still be friendly because it can be easy for all of us to share the same model that we all see is useful.

Theories tend to compete with rival explanations. In contrast, models tend to be relatively friendly toward each other's pictorializations. The point is not that competing with rivals is either better or worse than friendly welcoming of differences. Rather, one point is that theories and models seem to have substantial differences in that theories tend to compete with each other's explanations, whereas models tend to be friendly toward each other's pictorializations. Another point is that it seems cleaner and more convincingly easy to see which pictorialization is more useful for this specific use, and harder and looser to

try to determine convincingly which explanation is closest to the presumed truth.

Explanations

Citation of research-confirmed theoretical truths or pictorializing how something works

An experiential session starts by finding a scene of strong feeling in
order to be able to discover a deeper potential for experiencing.
Suppose that a questioner asks, 'How can a scene of strong feeling help
in discovering a deeper potential for experiencing?' or 'What is the relationship between a scene of strong feeling and a deeper potential for
experiencing?' The questioner is looking for an honest explanation.
However, the answers differ a great deal depending on whether the
mind-set is one of theories of truth or models of usefulness.

If the explanation is given in a mind-set of theories of truth, it ought
to be right, to cite theoretical truths, to cite things that are confirmed
by research, or at least research-confirmable. It ought to be made of
statements that are accepted, backed up by what is known, or solid
justifications, backed up with research-based evidence. Explain by
talking about what is known and accepted about the relationships
between emotions and deeper processes, about situational factors and
emotions, about emotional arousal and inner processes, about cognitions and situational involvement, and about the role of the situation
in eliciting inner processes.

When the explainer has a mind-set of models of use, rather than
theories of truth, there are at least two ways to explain; both are different from the way a theory of truth would go about it. One way is
to become somewhat practical. If the statement is that scenes of strong
feeling are the opening for discovering deeper potentials for experiencing, then one way to explain is to get down to the level of doing
this and that, and end with the discovery of deeper potentials for experiencing. 'How can a scene of strong feeling help in discovering a
deeper potential for experiencing?' The explanation is that starting
with a scene of strong feeling allows you to find the instant or moment
of peak feeling, and that actually living and being in the moment of
peak feeling can be done so as to discover the deeper potential for
experiences. Explanation is a matter of 'here is how it works'.

There is another way for explanation in the mind-set of models of use. It consists of providing a pictorialization, a seeable model or picture with the important preface that, if you think of or picture things in this way, it is easier and more sensible to use the scene of strong feeling to get a deeper potential for experiencing. The picture consists of a representation of the scene or situation, the potentials for experiencing that are more or less on the surface or thought of as deeper, and the feeling relationships between the potentials for experiencing on the surface and those that are thought of as deeper. This model is not thought of as 'true', but rather as a useful and helpful way to picture what is meant or portrayed by the relevant things for discovering the deeper potentials for experiencing.

When physicists use models to help explain or understand some physical phenomenon, they build or imagine a model that represents or simulates what the phenomenon is and how it works. Explanation or understanding means seeing the model and watching how it works. 'Understanding a physical phenomenon is the same thing as constructing a model that imitates that phenomenon. Consequently, understanding the nature of material things will be the same thing as imagining a mechanism that will represent or simulate the properties of bodies by its action' (Duhem, 1996, p. 55). Explaining or understanding what may be called a psychological phenomenon, such as the structure of personality or what is occurring in a scene of strong feeling, consists of building or imagining a pictorialized model that represents or simulates what that phenomenon is and how it works. How can we explain or understand the psychological phenomenon? The answer is to take a look at the pictorialized model. In other words, explanations can be substantially different, depending on whether your mind-set is one of theories of truth or models of usefulness.

Testing a theory's predictions or a model's predictions

It is traditional, in the long history of most sciences, to test the explanations provided by theories by generating predictions and to test those predictions carefully (Mill, 1862, Jevons, 1924, Ducasse, 1925). The worth or strength of the explanation depends in large part on whether or not the predictions are upheld.

This same principle is followed in testing explanations offered by theories in psychotherapy. Figure out what the explanation predicts and test those predictions. There may be explanations that are harder to test because they do not seem to provide testable predictions. 'Thus, when certain peculiarities in the work of an artist are explained as outgrowths of a specific type of neurosis, this observation may contain significant clues, but in general it does not afford a sufficient basis for a potential prediction of those peculiarities' (Hempel and Oppenheim, 1953, p. 324). Nevertheless, the aim in general is to test the theory's explanation by figuring out its prediction and then testing the prediction.

Models do not generally aim at testing their explanations. However, they do rely on trying to keep increasing the confidence that doing this leads to that, or that you can achieve that by doing this. Models seek to increase their predictability that this leads to that, or that you can achieve that by doing this. However, increasing these kinds of predictabilities has little or nothing to do with testing the explanations offered by models. Models are not in the business of testing their explanations, because they do not regard their explanations as true. They regard their explanations as helpful or useful, but not as true. Accordingly, models would probably not start with their explanations, try to generate testable predictions and test those predictions. That is the job of theories of truth, not models of usefulness.

Bioneurophysiological levels of explanation in theories and in models?

In seeking to explain many things, such as a headache or a person becoming gloomy or full of frenetic energy, theories of truth are inclined to think in terms of what they regard as more basic levels of explanation. Psychological constructs and variables are thought of as reducible to more basic ones. Generally, these are the constructs and variables of biology, neurology and physiology, although even more basic levels may be thought of such as a level of sheer physics (Schlick, 1953).

Theories of truth are inclined to think in terms of underlying, more basic levels of explanations so that the truer, more basic explanation lies at the level of biology, neurology, physiology or whatever is thought of as more basic than psychological constructs and variables.

Models are more inclined to think of explanations mainly in terms of how useful they are for the purposes or uses that they are to help achieve. They generally find it rather alien to think in terms of levels of explanations, with psychological constructs reducible to supposed-ly more basic biological, neurological or physiological constructs and variables.

Models are more inclined to think in terms of different conceptual systems, multiple systems of constructs and variables, each of which can offer its own explanation, with each explanation being relatively or not especially useful. Conceptual systems may be relatively pure, containing mainly psychological constructs and variables, or mainly biological, neurological, chemical, sociological, anatomical or any other kind of construct and variable. Conceptual systems may mix and match different kinds of constructs and variables. For models, the overriding consideration is whether the conceptual system is useful.

How do you choose which explanation is best?

Theories and models have different answers. Theories take this question quite seriously and count on a few ways of helping to choose which explanation is best. One consideration is whether the rival explanation comes from a field that is considered to be heavyweight or lightweight. If the theoretician thinks of microbiological or neuro-logical explanations as meaner, tougher and better than fluffy little psychological explanations, the theoretician doesn't have much of a problem deciding which explanation is best to explain the voice-like noises in the patient's head. A second consideration for theorists is which explanation includes parts that have been shown to be real and true by sound research (Hempel and Oppenheim, 1953). If one expla-nation includes the chemical structure of the relevant nerves, and the rival explanation is based on interjected archangels, then the theorist can make a decision between the two. A third consideration is which explanation seems to come closest to approximating the true state of things, the true nature of the phenomenon. Turn to research to see which explanation scores higher in predicting and controlling such noises in patient's heads.

Models do not bite their nails about seeking which explanation is best. They are observers, rather than contestants, in the game of choosing the best among different explanations. For models, the important consideration is which picture, which conceptualization, which model is more useful in whatever the aim or goal is, i.e. in accomplishing the use. If the person is especially upset and troubled by the noises in his head when he is pressured by his family to do what the family wants him to do, and if the intended aim is to be free of such painful scenes and feelings, that explanation is best which is most useful in helping to attain this goal. It seems that theories and models have rather different answers to the question of how to choose which explanation is best.

The theory of truth presents all sorts of evidence that its explanation is better than that of the model of usefulness. Its explanation is backed by lots of studies. Authorities accept its explanation. Great thinkers proposed the explanation. The explanation is grounded in a neurophysiological base. Students learn the explanation. Its truth is virtually unquestioned. With one eyebrow slightly raised, the theory of truth asks what evidence the model of usefulness can offer in defense of its obviously feeble explanation. 'Well, mine works!'

In general, models and theories seem to have different attitudes toward conceptual explanations. Models tend to favor their useful pictures over what they see as easy conceptual explanations. Theories tend to value what they think of as the true conceptual explanation.

What can a conceptualization provide?

Whether a conceptualization is more of a theory of truth, a model of usefulness or something else, it can make explanatory sense of things, or it can be correct or useful. The problem comes when presuming that if the conceptualization is any one of these, it must also be the other two. That presumption does not necessarily hold.

- Showing that a conceptualization can make explanatory sense of things does not mean that it is necessarily correct or useful. Most conceptualizations are accepted as making explanatory sense of things by the person who holds the conceptualization. Almost any event can be made sense of by lots of different conceptualizations. 'God's will' can make explanatory sense of lots of things. So can a psychoanalytic or a cognitive conceptual system.

- Showing that a conceptualization is correct does not necessarily mean that it is useful. That thing over there may be made sense of as being a white ceramic, but that is not necessarily much use to the thirsty person who is looking for a cup.

- Showing that a conceptualization is useful does not necessarily mean it is correct. It may work to have a conceptualization of this lock working by

> inserting the key and jiggling it because the lock opens when it giggles, but that is not necessarily the correct explanation of how locks work.

Psychotherapy often makes an error by presuming that, if its conceptualization can be shown to be able to make explanatory sense of things, or is correct or useful, it follows that it must also be the other two. That is almost always an error.

High-level conceptualization as the province for both theories of truth and models of usefulness

In psychotherapy, it is commonly accepted that conceptualization is almost exclusively the province of theories. Conceptualization is theorizing, and theorizing is conceptualizing. Instead of 'conceptual systems' of this or that, the field talks almost exclusively about theory, on the firm understanding that conceptualization is indeed the province of theory. There is virtually no other way of conceptualizing other than by theorizing. Theories seem to be convinced that they have the exclusive rights of engaging in conceptualization, and the field seems to agree.

Models beg to differ. From the perspective of models, theorizing is just one way of conceptualizing, providing conceptual frameworks, building conceptualization to make sense of things, to explain things, to understand things. Models modestly suggest that they offer an alternative way of conceptualizing, building conceptual systems. Models take exception to the common meaning of conceptualization as theorizing and theorizing as conceptualization.

Models suggest that model building can also provide conceptual systems that are powerful, exciting, sophisticated, far-reaching, profound, high level. Models provide an alternative conceptual system for what can be called models of personality, emotion, behavior, problem-solving, psychopathology, psychotherapy. There can be profoundly high-level models of where personality comes from in the first place, how and why change occurs, how to make sense of and use dreams, causality, craziness, personal transformation, the relationship between the brain and behavior, all psychological phenomena and behavior. Theories are one way to conceptualize. Models offer another way.

Indeed, models are ready to challenge theories as effective and useful ways of engaging in high-level conceptualization. Models believe that they are equal to or better than theories in providing conceptual understanding and explanation of the phenomena and events that are the subject matter of the field of psychotherapy. One of the main differences is that, where theories say that their conceptualizations are true, models are content to say that their conceptualizations are useful. At the very least, models offer a plausible and viable alternative avenue toward conceptualization. Theories are by no means the only, or perhaps even the best, way of conceptualizing.

Models versus theories in the use of science

If science is thought of as including research and careful thinking, reasoning, both models and theories enlist science. However, a case may be made that models and theories are inclined to enlist science for rather different purposes and in rather different ways. Models tend to enlist science to help discover ever new uses and ever new ways of helping to achieve their uses (e.g. Mahrer, 1985, 1988, 1996, 2003b; Mahrer and Boulet, 1999). Theories tend to enlist science to prove the truth of what theories believe is true.

In this section, the emphasis is on how models and theories are inclined to enlist science. The emphasis is not on how scientists in general enlist science, how researchers in general use science or how those who use rigorous thinking and reasoning tend to enlist science.

The moral of this section is that there can be different aims and purposes to science, exploration, research. Theories and models seem to use science, exploration and research for somewhat different aims and purposes.

> If theory does not have as its object the discovery of new experimental laws, still less does it have as an object the production of inventions useful in practical life. Theoretical speculations, experimental researches, and practical applications are three domains it is important not to confuse. Those who explore one of these domains are not required to make discoveries in the others.
>
> Duhem (1996, p. 27)

Science as an organizing framework for theories or for finding more and better uses in models

Theories depend on science to identify facts, to determine the empirical facts, to build the base of empirical knowledge. When this work is done well, theories can look at a display of empirically based principles, truths, factual knowledge. When this work is done exceedingly well, theories can enjoy a display of evidence-based laws.

Theories can then be developed to make sense of these facts, these laws. Theories are well suited to provide an organizing framework for scientific facts and laws. Experimental science can produce factual knowledge that can be developed into laws, and theories can organize, categorize and classify these laws: 'The aim of theory is to classify laws' (Duhem, 1996, p. 36).

In contrast, models are not there to search out factual knowledge, evidence-based principles, laws. The job of models is not to provide an organizing framework for factual knowledge, or to classify and categorize these laws. Instead, models are invented to serve their bottom-line uses. They enlist science mainly to help to discover more and more uses, and to discover, improve and advance better ways and means of accomplishing these uses.

Research in theories and models

Theories are made up of truths. Theories tell what is true. Theories are the buddies of the cumulative body of knowledge. What a theory says is to be true. If there is a question, the theory is to provide the answer: How did I get to be the person I am? What are the parts of my personality? Why do I sometimes seem to be forgetful? How come I am so attracted to this person and not especially attracted to that person? To a large extent, theories contain the answer. If a theory is a good theory, it has the truth.

To be scientifically upright, to show that it is worthy of respect, theories turn to science. Science confirms the truth of what the theory knows is true. Researchers test hypotheses and show that the theory is right, or at least well on the right track. A little fine-tuning here and there and the theory is ready to put on its dress uniform. Theories tell researchers to go ahead, test the theories out, confirm that the theories are truth-telling. If the theory has to be modified a little here and there, it is even more ready for confirmation. Test the theories now. In any case, the main reason for turning themselves over to researchers is to show that what they say is true. Go ahead, test my hypothesis.

In this sense, theories turn to science to confirm the truth of what the theories believe is true. Theories have beliefs. Science is a powerful way of showing the truth of those beliefs. The methodology is not as important as the beliefs. The actual hypothesis is not as important as the beliefs. The actual findings are not as important as the beliefs. The jewel is the belief that is believed to be true, rather than the actual hypothesis, the actual empirical findings. This is why it is so common for the reported 'finding' to be stated in terms of the confirmed belief, rather than in terms of the actual findings, the empirical data, the hypothesis that is tested. What is far more important is the belief that is confirmed to be true, the belief that is confirmed by the actual findings, the abstract belief rather that the facts. 'It is the interpretation of these facts and their transposition into the abstract symbolic world created by theories' (Duhem, 1996, p. 95). Science, including its methodology, design, testable hypotheses and findings, is put to work to confirm the truth of the belief that is believed to be true.

This is why it seems unfriendly, out of whack, wrong, misguided, to do research deliberately to try to show that the theory is wrong, to disconfirm, refute and even show that the theory is false (Popper, 1972a, 1972b, 1980). Doing research for this reason is dangerous. It is missing the point of why theories welcome researchers in the first place. If research is to show that the theory really speaks the truth, how could we possibly set out to do research that aims to show that the theory speaks falsehoods? This kind of research would not be especially popular with theories of truth.

Nevertheless, Popper insisted that the truly stringent way to show that a theory of truth is true is not by doing research to prove or confirm the theory's assertions, predictions or hypotheses. That way is not truly stringent, cannot be achieved with serious certainty, because there might always be a disproof. Instead, research on theories of truth should constantly strive to seek to disprove the theory, to show that it can be falsified, refuted.

Shift your mind-set over to models. Models offer themselves as helpful in your work. If you think this way, if you picture things this way, it can be easier for you to be clear on your aims, goals and uses, and you will probably be better able to attain your aims, goals and uses. Models are convenient and useful tools for your work, your job. Models, therefore, are not geared to spew a stream of truths. They are not here to tell what is true.

Accordingly, models are not especially inclined to hire or inspire researchers to show that its truths are really true. Models do not ask researchers to confirm its truths, to test its truths, to validate or verify that what it theorizes as true is really true. Nor would models be especially inclined to ask researchers to try to disconfirm its professed truths, to show that its hypotheses are wrong, false, refuted. Models do not produce truths that researchers are to stamp as either true or false.

Instead, models turn to researchers to ask them to discover better and better ways of doing the job, accomplishing the goal, achieving the use. If the aim or goal is to be free of a painful feeling in a painful situation, models ask researchers to discover better and better ways of accomplishing that aim or goal. Models foster discovery-oriented research (Mahrer, 2003b) to help find better and better ways of accomplishing the job. For models, science discovers more and more about how to accomplish the uses. For theories, science confirms that the theories are indeed true or at least getting closer to the truth.

How models view the basic truths of theories

Theories love to make pronouncements about basic truths, and that these are really basic truths about the way things really are. Theories love to think of their basic truths as arising out of science and tested by science. They love to think of their basic truths as serious, somber, scientific approximations of the ways that things really are, e.g. theories assert that there is a lawfulness and order to psychological phenomena, that there really are such things as mental illnesses and diseases, needs and drives, addictive personalities, that biological, neurological and physiological events and variables are basic to psychological events and variables.

When models look at the things that theories say are true, models see theorists inventing, concocting, creating constructions of the world, the way people are, the pieces and bits of 'personality', the way that people change. Models see theorists as engaged in personal world building, as creative artists constructing personal worlds.

What gets this personal world building started and keeps it going? What fuels the theory building that theorists are engaged in? According to models, the theorist builds the kind of personal world, their theory, because it is important for the theorist to construct that particular kind of world, that particular theory. In other words, the theorist builds that particular theory because of the theorist's own personal hopes and wishes that this is the way the theorist hopes and wishes things are. The theorist hopes and wishes that the world of psychological things is really lawful and orderly. The theorist hopes and wishes that there are such things as needs and drives, that there are growth forces and addictive personalities, that neurological and physiological events and variables are basic to psychological events and variables. Theorists build basic truths because of theorists' own hopes and wishes that these things are really true.

Proposition: is it true or is it useful?

Here are some propositions: biological, neurological, physiological and chemical events and variables are basic to psychological events and variables. The brain is a basic determinant of human behavior. Input from the past is stored in the brain and used in the form of concepts to process present input. Human beings have inborn, intrinsic biological and psychological needs, drives, instincts and motivations; these include needs and drives for survival, sex, aggression, object seeking, contact comfort. There are biopsychological stages of human growth and development. Responses followed by satisfying consequences tend to be strengthened; responses followed by unsatisfying consequences tend to be weakened. Causal determinants of human behavior generally lie in antecedent events. The therapist–client relationship is a prerequisite to successful psychotherapy. Insight and understanding are prerequisites to successful psychotherapy. Clients with low ego strength and inadequate defenses may be harmed by excessive stress in psychotherapy.

These are just a small sample from an almost unending list of propositions. Faced with such a proposition, a theory's almost natural tendency would be to ask if it is true. The theory is ready to use science to see if the proposition is indeed true. The theory is designed to investigate the proposition, to launch empirical studies to see if the proposition holds up to carefully controlled empirical research. If a large body of rigorous studies shows that the proposition is indeed true, the proposition is informed that it is indeed true, and it is supported by research. Theories are mightily inclined to go to work to see whether or not the proposition is true.

Faced with the same proposition, models are not inclined to ask if the proposition is true. Models are not especially inclined to enlist science to check out the truth of the proposition. Instead, models are much more inclined to ask whether such a proposition is useful. If I think this way, what effect will it have on getting what I am trying to get, on achieving the aims and goals I am trying to achieve? Is thinking this way helpful or not especially helpful in the uses that I have?

Models tend to enlist science, as well as careful logic and reasoning, to answer questions such as these. Answering these questions convincingly usually means calling on means and methods that are careful and rigorous. Those who use models, when faced with a new proposition, may well ask whether inclusion of that proposition makes a helpful difference in the work, in achieving the uses.

If the answer is no, the model user might consider whether or not the proposition helps to organize the propositions that are already in the model. Seeing whether inclusion of the new proposition makes a helpful difference in the work usually calls for doing some sort of science. Seeing whether inclusion of the new proposition helps make the present propositions better organized, cleaner, prettier, simpler, etc., usually calls for careful reasoning and logic rather than some kind of scientific research.

In any case, theories and models have rather different reactions to a new proposition. Theories ask if it is true. Models ask if it is useful.

Proving the truth of the component parts of theories and models

Theories tend to believe that their pieces and parts are real, true, exist. There really and truly are things like an unconscious, primary emotions, metacognitions, efficacy motivations, a need for affiliation, a growth force. Theories can be deadly serious about enlisting science to prove that these things really and truly exist. If you question the existence of an unconscious or metacognitions, those who know can quote the relevant research studies. For theories, that is one important thing that science is for.

A psychoanalytic researcher can be extremely adept at using sophisticated research methodologies and tools to lend research support for the solid existence of psychoanalytic things such as a superego, libido and unconscious impulses. Do controlled experiments. Carefully deduce from the theory testable hypotheses. Assemble a body of well-done research findings so that the existence of psychoanalytic things and parts can sit more confidently. Science is there to help provide secure trust and confidence in the parts that comprise the theories.

But not for models. Models are made up of invented parts that are invented because they are convenient fictions. They are fictions. It would be virtually absurd for an experiential model to hire researchers to prove the truth of deeper potentials for experiencing, to show that they really exist. Models may include things such as an unconscious, primary emotions, metacognitions, efficacy motivations, needs for affection and even a growth force. However, these are, in models, invented convenient fictions, not presumably real and true things. Models would almost certainly not set out to do studies aimed at proving the 'truth' of these invented convenient fictions.

Those who hold to a theory of truth know that a part is good if it can be tested, if it can be shown to be confirmed or disconfirmed, proved or disproved. Both the proponents of a psychoanalytic 'unconscious' and their critics tend to share the mind-set that, if there is such a thing as a psychoanalytic unconscious, it can lend itself to confirmation or disconfirmation. It is on this point that proponents can be defensive and critics can strike home. If there truly are unconscious forces at work, it can be exceedingly hard for researchers to know what they are, because they are unconscious, and it is exceedingly hard to disconfirm unconscious factors because, again, they may be at work without our knowing that they are at work. For both proponents and critics, this is a serious issue, but it arises, and makes sense, in a mind-set of a theory of truth about a part such as the psychoanalytic 'unconscious'.

If we switch over to a mind-set of models of usefulness, the above serious issue diffuses away, becomes a non-issue of silly irrelevance. It is replaced by an issue of whether or not, to what degree, the notion of an 'unconscious' is a useful notion to have in your conceptual system (e.g. Holmes and Lindley, 1989).

Where theories of truth are in deadly earnest as they work hard at trying to prove the truth of their pieces and parts, models of usefulness stand by, shaking their heads from side to side, respectfully declining to enter the fray, and much preferring to rely on careful ways of seeing whether or not their parts are especially useful.

A theory as a set of basic assumptions and a model as simple pictorialization

There are starting points or foundational blocks to a theory. They may be referred to as their fundamental propositions, their basic principles, their basic assumptions. To qualify as rigorous, a theory should be able to put its basic assumptions on the table.

Another test of the rigor of a theory is that its array of principles and propositions should be deducible or derivable from the set of basic assumptions. Indeed, you have distilled the smallest number of basic assumptions when the principles and propositions can be shown to be deduced and derived from the smallest set of basic propositions (Nagel, 1953). Prime examples of being able to apply this test are in the theories of mathematics and logic.

In models, the story is quite different. Reduced to its simplest form, a model is a simple pictorialization, e.g. the simplest form of a psychoanalytic model is a pictorialization of id, ego and superego. The simplest form of the experiential model is a pictorialization of potentials for experiencing and their relationships (Mahrer, 1989, 1996/2004). There is no lattice of theoretical principles and propositions, logically related to each other and resting on a set of basic assumptions.

Submission to scientific testing or challenging the belief as an overblown myth

Most theories stand tall, one hand on their heart, eyes uplifted and solemnly recite their oath: 'Theories dutifully submit themselves to rigorous scientific testing and examination.' Theories have confidence in themselves because they do the right thing, namely they survive the test of rigorous science. If any of their parts fail the test of scientific scrutiny, the theory proudly lets go of that part. Theories are continuously at work testing and examining their parts, their fundamental propositions. A good theory regards its principles and propositions as 'open to revision, and is always ready to modify or abandon them if evidence should render them doubtful' (Feigl, 1953, p. 13). One of the highest aims of research is to examine a theory's principles and propositions to see whether they are flawed and poor or whether they emerge as pure and sound.

If there are problems in testing large theories, these problems can be solved, but make sure that testing is upheld and carried out. After all, there is no plausible alternative to testing hypotheses (see Mahrer, 1988, 2003b). Accordingly, if there are problems in testing grand theories, solve the problems and get on with the testing of hypotheses:

> I would argue that counselling researchers should not be involved in the business of testing such grand theories. Rather, psychologists need to develop smaller theories with testability in mind.

> Gelso (1991, p. 212)

In any case, theories of truth stand ready to be tested by researchers to prove that they are worthy, good, sound, and to use research findings to become even more worthy, good, sound.

Models challenge those beliefs. They may simply know theories too well to accept such garbage, or they may be dyed in the wool misbelievers, miscreants, unbelieving heretics. In any case, models are inclined to listen to what theories portray, fold their arms across their chests, tilt their heads to one side, raise an eyebrow and say: 'Come on, theories; it is garbage, a collective myth.' Models look through history for three or five notable instances when the leaders of a theory did the right thing and publicly announced that, after years of scientific scrutiny, they are taking the momentous step of declaring their theory as failing the test, and therefore declaring their theory as wrong, inadequate and to be scrapped. It would be very hard to find solid evidence that theories submit themselves to scientific scrutiny, and dutifully accept and take the right and proper action on the basis of the findings.

Indeed, say models, theories uphold the opposite injunction. Those who belong to the theoretical family shall not seriously question, scrutinize or examine the theory. It is not permitted to expose its principles and propositions as perhaps false, wrong, lacking. Our theory shall not be exposed to the real possibility of disconfirmation, refutation, falsification (see Fuller, 1996, Popper, 1972a). That is blasphemous. Any family member who dares to do that is in deep trouble.

However, scientists are encouraged by their theories to test, poke, examine and scrutinize other theories. With sufficient scientific evidence, one theory can then tell the rival theory that it is scientifi-cally duty bound to do the honorable thing: resign, declare itself defeated, disproved, disconfirmed, falsified, wrong. Here is the over-whelming scientific evidence. Does the attacked theory dutifully sacrifice itself? Does it even sacrifice the attacked basic proposition or principle? Not very likely. Almost as a rule, the attacked theory pro-tects and retains the attacked theory or proposition or principle by using the clever ploy of pinning the blame on such vulnerable things as the inadequate hypothesis, the inadequate sample, research design, procedure, statistics, logic and reasoning, on the safely sacrificial aux-iliary premises, and lesser principles and secondary propositions around the coveted and immunized precious theory, principle or proposition (Duhem, 1953, 1962, Quine, 1961, Lakatos, 1978, Chalmers, 1982, Gorman, 1996, Mahrer, 2000).

Here is a test of the theory's willingness to abide by the test of sci-ence. Ask a theory:

> You are truly willing to submit your theory, your hallowed principle or propositions to the test of science? All right, then please spell out the reasonable evidence or grounds (research or logical or clinical or whatever) that you would accept as sufficient for you to give up your theory, your principle or proposition.

> Mahrer (1995a, 1996/2004, 1997, 1998, 2000)

The evidence or grounds are reasonable if those who are outside the theory and are going to assemble the evidence or grounds regard them as reasonable. The trouble is that most models know that most theo-ries fail this test. Most theories are absolutely unwilling to state the reasonable grounds they would accept as sufficient to abandon their theory, principle or proposition. Put to the test, most theories do not submit themselves to such serious scientific testing, and models know this.

Most theories of truth proudly identify what they accept as a solid basic truth, e.g. a theory may hold that there is a reality out there, that some things are real, that large parts of the external world are real. However, these theories rarely set forth the reasonable grounds, research, logic or whatever that would be sufficient for them to aban-don their precious basic truth. On the other hand, these theories attack rival theories of truth that hold a rival basic truth, e.g. people con-struct and build their worlds, so there is no external reality. What is interesting is that the attack usually involves assembling scientific evidence, research, logical and otherwise, to show that the rival basic truth is wrong, poor, flawed, inferior, and the rival is supposed to acknowledge that it is wrong, poor, flawed, inferior.

Models watch this kind of attack in a kind of playful bewilderment. 'You refuse to allow your basic truth to face the test of laying out the reasonable evidence you would accept as sufficient to give up your basic truth, right? Yet you attack a rival basic truth and honestly expect that the rival theory of truth is to face the same test that you declare as not applicable to you? You expect your rival to do what you would not do? How very interesting.'

And yet, there can be some basic notions and ideas that most theories and most models would accept as not especially vulnerable to this kind of careful investigation, scrutiny, inquiry. Here is what I mean: most theories and models accept that some basic notions and ideas are outside the boundaries of scientific testing, partly because you need these basic notions and ideas just to be able to play the game of theories and models, e.g. you may start with some propositions that are to be accepted as unquestioned eternal truths, beyond the need for scientific testing, e.g. through two points in space there always passes one and only one straight line. Or you begin with some basic definitions that, being definitions, are outside the stuff of research inquiry, e.g. in the field of mathematics, it is accepted that $3 + 2 = 5$.

> And this is so because the symbols '3 + 2' and '5' denote the same number: they are synonomous by virtue of the fact that the symbols '2', '3', '5', and '+' are *defined* (or tacitly understood) in such a way that the above identity holds as a consequence of the meaning attached to the concepts involved in it.
>
> Hempel (1953, p. 149)

To get into operation, it is often necessary to start with some things that are simply accepted. They may be called definitions, theorems, postulates or simply game rules. They are understood to be outside research examination (Campbell, 1953, Duhem, 1953). The problem, according to models, is that most theories crowd far too many of their basic notions and ideas into the sanctuary of research-immune definitions, theorems, postulates or game rules (Mahrer, 2000, 2003a). Theories do a good public-relations job of claiming to submit themselves to scientific testing, and they can do so because they are clever at handing over a very small proportion of their theoretical parts, and largely unimportant parts at that, to scientific scrutiny.

Models do not claim that their conceptual systems are true, so they are in a good position to see that, when theories proudly proclaim that they dutifully submit themselves to scientific testing, theories are not especially telling the truth. Models see that proclamation as pretty much of an overblown myth. They are not especially impressed when theories insist that they submit themselves to scientific testing, when theories insist that they follow the scientific method of deducing hypotheses that are tested to see if they hold up or fail to hold up. Instead, models suggest, theories are used far more commonly to justify, to provide a basis for, what is believed and what is carried out in the name of the theory. If a psychotherapist believes that women are basically different from men, the psychotherapist can justify that belief with a fitting theory. If a psychotherapist believes that children should not be raised by gay parents, the psychotherapist can justify that action by some fitting theory. Models charge that psychotherapists are inclined to use theories to justify their beliefs and their actions, and only rarely, if ever, to deduce hypotheses to test the truth of the theories. Models charge that psychotherapists merely proclaim that they submit their theories to scientific testing. The main use of theories, proponents of models charge, is to justify the beliefs and the actions that psychotherapists have and carry out.

In general, theories proudly proclaim that they dutifully submit themselves to scientific testing. Models bring up a fair number of issues that challenge such a claim. Models say that such a proclamation is an overblown myth and models make a fair case to back up their charge.

Hypothesis testing in theories and models

Theories portray themselves, and like to think of themselves, as logical lattices from which hypotheses can be deduced. If the hypothesis is confirmed, the theory is supposed to be strengthened. If the hypothesis is not confirmed, the theory is supposed to be weakened.

There are at least four problems that suggest that this is not true and that instead theories are essentially immune from the results of such hypothesis testing:

1. In psychotherapy, few if any theories consist of such logical lattices. There is little or no basis for a process of logical reasoning to start from a theory and to culminate in the logical deduction of a testable hypothesis.

2. As there is no such logical lattice, neither the confirmation nor the disconfirmation of a hypothesis can point toward a particular part of the logical latticework. Even in many other fields with theories made up of logical lattices, confirmation or disconfirmation of a hypothesis may reflect well or poorly on the theory as a whole, but rarely does it point directly toward a particular piece in the logical latticework. If the hypothesis is not confirmed or is disconfirmed, the findings rarely point out the specific culprit. 'If the predicted phenomenon does not appear, it is not the disputed proposition alone that is shown to be wanting – there is at least one error among all the propositions used to predict this phenomenon. But experiment does not tell us where this error lies' (Duhem, 1996, pp. 82–83).

3. In psychotherapy, almost all hypotheses may be said to be generally consistent or inconsistent with some theory, to bear some degree of goodness of fit with some theory, rather than being a product of careful reasoning down a logical latticework, so that the findings are directly connected with a given piece or part of the logical latticework. Accordingly, the findings from testing a hypothesis may help the theory feel better or worse, but the theory need not worry that any part of the theory has to be changed. It is the theory as a whole that smiles at or worries about the results of testing hypotheses.

4. In psychotherapy, there is no logical latticework of principles. There is usually a loose theory and a hypothesis that is loosely connected to the loose theory. Suppose that an impressive and insistent crowd of studies demands some sort of change in the theory. Does that theory have much to worry about? Is the danger serious? Not really.

Between the theory and the hypothesis, there is typically a bureaucracy of minor officials, lower-level officers, technocrats, clerks, auxiliary principles and secondary propositions. These make up a protective moat, an effective filler and barrier, between the slightly vulnerable theory and the defeated hypothesis. If something has to be let go, take the blame, be altered or fired, it is almost certain that the culprit is some easily sacrificed and dispensable auxiliary principle or secondary proposition. The theory can sleep without worry. It is safe. It is essentially immune.

What about models? Models do not have to fret about losing the hypothesis-testing contest, because there are at least two reasons why these contests do not even exist in their world. One reason is that models do not aspire to or pretend to be lattices of clear reasoning. They merely offer helpful pictorializations and conveniently useful notions and ideas. A second reason is that models do not do research to test the truth, to confirm or disconfirm the truth, of carefully deduced hypotheses. Instead of testing the truth of their principles and beliefs, models do research mainly to advance and carry forward the uses that they were created to help achieve.

The case is that theories are essentially immune from the results of hypothesis testing, whereas models have little or no reason to deduce, formulate or test such hypotheses.

Testing hypotheses about the true nature of things, versus looking for new and better ways of achieving uses

What are theories for? What do theories do? 'One kind of answer to this question is that theories do, or aim to, describe what the world is really like . . . From the realist point of view, the kinetic theory of gases describes what gases are really like' (Chalmers, 1982, p. 146). In our field, theories strive to get at the true nature, structure and organization of things such as cognitions, depression, emotions, egos, psychopathology, anxiety, paranoia, stages of development, obsessive behavior, criminal behavior, sexual behavior, prosocial behavior, problem-solving behavior.

Theories generate hypotheses about the true nature, structure and organization of these things, and theories enlist science to test these hypotheses carefully and rigorously. Theories know that there is a single true nature, structure and organization of these things, and vie with one another to see which theory comes closest to grasping and approximating the true nature, structure and organization of these things. Theories yield hypotheses about what the world is really like, how it really works, and science is used to see whether the theories are right or close or substantially wrong.

The scientific testing of a theory's hypothesis is supposed to be mercilessly fair, rigorous, hard. If a theory is working on a new idea, a fledgling notion that is still on its baby legs, it is not ready for tough scientific testing (Mitroff, 1974). Science is then softer, gentler, kinder. But when the idea is ready for grown-up testing, it must be mature enough to be subjected to the rigors of tough scientific testing.

Theories generate and test hypotheses in order to frame laws about the true nature, structure and organization of things. The laws allow the scientist to explain and predict what things are like and how they work. 'The scientist seeks to establish laws relating his concepts or variables because they make possible explanation and prediction' (Spence, 1953, p. 577). Research is good because it enables the scientist to frame laws about the true nature, structure and organization of things.

If we switch over to models, models do not think of things as having some sort of true nature, structure and organization. It would be a fruitless quest to set out to find the true nature, structure and organization of primary emotions or cognitive schemata, or the intrapsychic dynamics of someone with a borderline psychosis. Models don't even bother trying to enlist science in what models regard as a fruitless quest, a quest for the true nature, structure and organization of a mythological fiction. 'Perhaps the greatest advantage of what I thus take to be the correct logical description of models is that it keeps one from indulging in a certain kind of dilettante speculation about the "real nature" of the physical universe' (Bergmann, 1953, p. 486) or, I would add, the universe in which most theories of psychotherapy live, with their mind-set for getting at the true nature, structure and organization of the supposed things in that universe.

In models, the mind-set is quite different, and the uses and aims of science are different, and therefore the methods of science are different (Mahrer, 2003b). Models are on the lookout for better and better ways of achieving their current batch of uses. If the aim, goal or use is to free the person of the state of tension and anxiety, we may have some reasonably effective ways of doing this. Science is enlisted to discover better and better methods. If the valued use is knowing what the other person is feeling, we may have sophomoric baby methods of accomplishing this. Science is enlisted to discover much better methods.

In addition, models enlist science to discover new uses. They know what can be achieved in and through sessions of psychotherapy. By carefully enlisting science, models can discover new uses, valued and impressive uses. In a single session, science may show us how a person may undergo an enormously impressive shift into becoming the qualitatively new person that he or she is capable of becoming. Here is an exciting newly discovered use of a single session. In a single session, the person is now free of the deadly cancer that had been consuming him or her. Here is another newly discovered use of what can occur in a single session. Furthermore, science can discover methods for how to accomplish these new and exciting uses.

Theories use a set of scientific ways and means to test hypotheses about the true nature, structure and organization of things, of the world. In contrast, models use what is ordinarily a substantially different set of scientific ways and means to discover new uses for psychotherapy, and for better and better ways of achieving these uses.

Trying to get at the true nature of things, versus the value of discovery

A theory will try to help understand how real things work, what their true nature, structure and organization is. The theory will help a person figure out how a clock works, how a battery-charger works, how a lamp works, what their true nature, structure and organization are. A theory can help a person to figure out what a seed is made of, how a spider creates its web, how a bird's wings work. A theory starts with things that are real, and studies their nature, structure and organization. A theory starts with things that are considered real, things such as emotions, anxiety, cognitions and egos, and the theory uncovers their true nature, structure and organization, how they work.

In psychotherapy, models know that the things they use are not real. They are convenient fictions. Models know that their actual uses can be considered real, but the things that models count on as instruments and tools, to obtain those uses, are not real. Models of psychotherapy know that emotions are convenient fictions, not real things. The same holds for anxiety, cognitions and egos. These things are convenient fictions, not real things. Therefore, as far as models are concerned, they would not try to employ science to get the true nature, structure and organization of convenient fictions such as emotions, anxiety, egos or cognitions. Models would instead decline to mount research programs to dig into and uncover the nature, structure and organization of all those many things that models know are merely convenient fictions. Inventing these things may be helpful and useful and convenient, even though none of these things is considered real as far as models are concerned.

Probability statements in theories and models

If a theory is good, it can tell what the world is really like. If a theory knows what the world is really like, the theory can produce probability statements, predictions, about what happens. If you do this, here is what happens in the real world. The event will happen with a probability of 0.20 or 0.67 or 0.98, and the confidence value of this prediction is 0.55 or 1.00. This meaning 'of probability is factual and empirical, and it says something about the facts of nature, and hence must be based upon empirical procedure, the observation of relevant facts' (Carnap, 1953, p. 447).

In models, the meaning of probability is equally factual and empirical, equally based on empirical procedure, the observation of empirical facts. However, the big difference is that in theories probability statements say something about the facts of nature, whereas in models they say something about the relationship between methods and their intended uses. This method is effective in achieving this use with a probability of 0.87. The probability that this method will achieve that use is 0.75 or 0.34 or 0.90.

The carefulness and stringency of probability statements may well be comparable in theories and models. Both theories and models may employ probability statements. However, in theories the probability statements tell about the real world, what it is really like and how it really works. In models, the probability statements tell about the degree of strength or confidence in the relationship between methods and the uses for which the methods may be used.

Which conceptual system is better?

Theories of truth are inclined to agree that the better theory is the one that comes closest to approximating reality, to portraying or getting at what is true. One theory of light may hold that light consists of projectiles emitted with extreme velocity. A rival theory may hold that light consists of vibrations with waves propagated in an elastic medium. If they are thought of as theories of truth, one can be shown to be better by showing that it provides a better approximation of reality. The same generally applies to comparing a psychoanalytic theory, a cognitive theory and an existential theory.

Models of usefulness are inclined to suggest two answers to the question of how to tell which model is better than the others. One answer is that which one is better depends on being more careful in framing the question. If the question is: 'Which one is better for this particular use?', it is important to see whether both are models for the same particular use. If they are not, it is virtually impossible to compare them to see which one is better. If the two models of light are used for different purposes, different uses, they have a hard time being compared with one another.

On the other hand, if they are both models for the same use, they can be compared; one can be found to be better. The question is: 'Which model is more useful for this particular use?' That question can be answered, and one can be seen as better, i.e. more useful, than the others.

The power of prediction versus the value of discovery

In theories, prediction is very important. Theories tend to enlist science to test predictions, and the ability to predict is a worthy test of the mettle of a theory. So theories do their best to be able to predict, and to elevate themselves by using science to show that their predictions are on the mark. As far as theories are concerned, science is mainly a rigorous way of testing out predictions, hypotheses, and, if the predictions are upheld, that means the theory is a good one.

As theories largely aim at capturing what the world is really like, a fine theory can even predict things that haven't been found yet, that haven't occurred yet. These future events can be predicted because the theory knows what the world is truly like, the rules and principles that govern the world. This is high-level prediction. A truly fine theory:

> . . . can forecast the occurrence of events the likes of which have never before been encountered. Thus, generalizations based upon periodicities exhibited by the characteristics of chemical elements then known enabled Mendeleef in 1871 to predict the existence of a certain new element and to state correctly various properties of that element as well as of several of its compounds; the element in question, germanium, was not discovered until 1886.
>
> Hempel and Oppenheim (1953, p. 335)

Models are not geared to show that they are true. They are not disposed toward approximating the real and true nature and operations of the real and true world. They do not enlist science to show that the models are true or truly depict the real world. In other words, models do not enlist science to test out rigorously generated predictions.

Models are born and raised to help discover new things, and science is enlisted gratefully to help in that search (Mahrer, 2003b). However, in the grand search for the discovery of new things, the generation and testing of predictions do not play an especially important role. In fact, if a person is fascinated with prediction, that person ought to join the theory camp because models pay very little attention to it.

Sophistication of research tools versus the value of discovery

Almost every year produces more sophisticated scientific tools, research designs, measuring instruments, research hardware, software, computer technology, statistics. As far as models are concerned, these ever more sophisticated research tools are valued and respected. However, the worth of science is not so much in the sophistication of the research tools.

Rather, the bottom-line test of research tools is whether they are of actual use in discovering new and better uses, and ways of achieving these uses. The researcher has a particular aim or use in mind. In the actual session, we may value the person's becoming free of the painful state of worry, depression, tension. Can the more sophisticated scientific research tool help the researcher find new and better ways of achieving this end or use in the session? Can the more sophisticated scientific research tool discover new and better changes, uses or accomplishments in the session? For models, the worth of sophisticated research tools lies more in answering these questions than merely in the degree to which the researcher includes sophisticated research tools in the research.

Competition with rival truths versus respect for others' beliefs

Theories are drawn toward elevating themselves over other theories, toward defeating their rivals, toward subjugating their rivals. Everyone has to bow down and worship the truths of the reigning theory. 'We must all live in the same world, therefore everyone must think like me, at least when they are thinking right' (Fuller, 1996, p. 37). In this struggle, science can be a powerful weapon, a powerful force.

Theories can enlist science to support the truths of a theory. It is called research support, research validation, confirmation. Research studies show the truth of what we say is true. The winning theory is the one with the strongest research support. It can enlist science by ennobling the theory's truths into laws. What we believe is true must be worshipped as true because it is a law. Everyone must salute our law of effect because it is simply a law, a truth not to be questioned. Science has given us the law of effect, and all theories must obey the laws that science pronounces as laws.

Theories can also enlist science by placing and keeping truths in the hallowed cumulative body of knowledge. Everyone must accept the truths in the scientific cumulative body of knowledge, especially when they are the truths of our theory. Theories can enlist science to lend its weight to what the theory holds as its basic truths, fundamental propositions, foundational postulates. Science accepts that the brain is a basic determinant of human behavior, that there are mental illnesses and diseases, that the therapist–client relationship is a prerequisite to psychotherapeutic change.

Theories know how powerful science can be in helping a theory to defeat its rival theories, to subjugate rivals, to force rival theories to accept what the reigning theory holds as its truths. Get science on your side. It helps in the war.

Models are not even in the contest. They regard other models as likewise emphasizing usefulness. Models are typically respectful of the beliefs of other models. As models value usefulness, and as they comprise beliefs, convenient fictions, and not truths, they tend to have no basis for getting into the grim war games of establishing laws, building and maintaining cumulative bodies of knowledge, framing basic truths and trying to enlist science to validate, confirm, uphold and support models' beliefs and convenient fictions. Models have little or no basis for seeing other models as rivals, for trying to get other models to accept and bow down to the model's beliefs, to impose their beliefs on other models. There is such a big difference between the world in which theories live and the world in which models live.

As far as theories are concerned, the truth of the assertions of one theory can entail the falsity of assertions made in another theory. If our assertions of truth conflict, one must ultimately be shown to be true and the other as not so true, or even false. Theories have trouble accepting that 'the truth of the assertions of one approach does not necessarily entail the falsity of assertions made in another approach' (Geer and O'Donohue, 1989, p. 14). Models have little or no trouble here. One model's belief that the thing is ceramic is not necessarily threatened or damaged by other model's beliefs that the thing is white or that it is a cup.

Theories tend to try to prove that their insistence on what is true is really true. Theories do research to prove, confirm, verify that this thing is really and truly ceramic. Theories can then proudly assert that the body of studies tends to show that it is really and truly ceramic. The idea, in the mind-set of theories, is that, if the thing can be shown to be ceramic, that body of research means that the thing is therefore not white or a cup. This is the way that theories tend to think.

Models do not have such a mind-set. In contrast, models say that, no matter how much research can be shown to confirm that the thing is ceramic, this does not mean: (1) the thing is only ceramic, i.e. it is not also white and a cup, (2) the thing is more ceramic than it is white or a cup or (3) calling that thing ceramic is more useful than calling it white or a cup. Therefore, models are disinclined to launch a research program aimed at proving, confirming, verifying that this thing is ceramic, or any other theoretical assertion of truth, or any other hypothesis of what this thing is really and truly like.

Theories enlist science in their wars with rival theories. Models live in a world in which there is more likely to be respect for the beliefs of other models. Here is a grand and common enlistment of science that is essentially declined by most models.

Chapter 4

Conclusions and invitations

The main purpose for trying to identify some conclusions is to pave the way toward taking some actions. These actions are given as 'invitations', but they are really invitations to take some active steps toward one way of helping to bring about a revolution in the field of psychotherapy.

A case is made for a distinction between what may be called 'theories of truth' and 'models of usefulness' in the field of psychotherapy theory, research and practice. There are, so the case holds, basic and fundamental ways in which theories of truth and models of usefulness can be distinguished from one another. I have tried to describe some of these ways.

In the field of psychotherapy, this distinction produces a somewhat embarrassing division in which virtually all the conceptual systems wave the flag of theories of truth, whereas only a token few nervously display little flags of models of usefulness. Indeed, with the exception of Mahrer's experiential model, and a few other, equally straggly exceptions, the entire field of psychotherapy seems to be almost wall-to-wall theories of truth.

A case is presented that models of usefulness offer some preferential features in comparison with theories of truth:

1. Models are especially useful in providing pictorialized conceptualizations that help get the job done.

2. Models are generally more open to improvement or replacement than are theories.

3. Theories rely on a base of 'foundational truths'; models decline a base of 'foundational truths', and instead define themselves as positions on basic issues or answers to basic questions.

4. Models offer ways of resolving some of the unresolved problems of theories.

5. Models offer useful pictures over easy conceptual explanations; theories value trying to find true conceptual explanations.
6. Models enlist science to discover new uses and better ways of achieving them; theories enlist science to show that they are true.

Each of the preferential features of models over theories can open the way to powerful and revolutionary implications for the field of psychotherapy, for psychotherapy conceptualization, research, education and training, and especially practice. The invitation is for those psychotherapists with cordially open mind-sets (1) to know and appreciate these implications, (2) to take actual steps toward helping to bring about these implications and (3) actually to adopt models of usefulness.

For the field as a whole, perhaps the more practical and realistic invitation is to reserve a little room for models of usefulness. The invitation is just a friendly first step, rather than an aggressively hostile takeover. Without interfering with the near universality of theories of truth, the plea is for the field to be a little welcoming toward reserving a little room. This heartfelt invitation is extended to those psychotherapy researchers, practitioners, philosophers of science, thinkers–conceptualizers and teacher–trainers whose mind-sets can be at least a little bit open to models of usefulness.

If a little room can be reserved for models of usefulness, if the field can achieve a fair understanding and appreciation of what models of usefulness can offer, and if some psychotherapy theorists, researchers, teacher–trainers and especially practitioners can actually achieve the shift into models of usefulness, then I believe that the way is open for psychotherapy to take a grand and glorious step forward. This is a revolution that can be.

References

Achinstein, B. (1965). Theoretical models. British Journal for the Philosophy of Science, 16, 102–120.

Apostel, L. (1961). Towards the formal study of models in the non-formal sciences. In: Freudenthal, H. (ed.), The Concept and the Role of the Model in Mathematics and Natural and Social Sciences. New York: Gordon & Breach, 1–38.

Ariew, R. and Barker, P. (1996). Pierre Duhem: Essays in the history and philosophy of science. Indianapolis, In: Hackett, vii–xx.

Bacon, F. (1889). Novum organum. Oxford: Oxford University Press (original work published 1620).

Bartley, W.W. (1988). Theories of rationality. In: Radnitsky, G. and Bartley, W.W. (eds), Evolutionary Epistemology, Rationality, and the Sociology of Knowledge. LaSalle, Il: Open Court, 205–216.

Bergmann, G. (1953). The logic of quanta. In: Feigl, H. and Brodbeck, M. (eds), Readings in the Philosophy of Science. New York: Appleton-Century-Crofts, 475–508.

Bunge, M. (1972). Toward a philosophy of technology. In: Mitcham, C.M. and Mackay, R. (eds), Philosophy and technology. New York: Free Press, 62–76.

Campbell, N.R. (1953). The structure of theories. In: Feigl, H. and Brodbeck M. (eds), Readings in the Philosophy of Science. New York: Appleton-Century-Crofts, 288–308.

Carnap, R. (1953). The two concepts of probability. In: Feigl, H. and Brodbeck M. (eds), Readings in the Philosophy of Science. New York: Appleton-Century-Crofts, 438–455.

Chalmers, A.F. (1982). What is this Thing called Science? Queensland, Australia: University of Queensland Press.

Ducasse, C.J. (1925). Explanation, mechanism, and technology. Journal of Philosophy, 22, 150–155.

Duhem, P. (1953). Physical theory and experiment. In: Feigl, H. and Brodbeck M. (eds), Readings in the Philosophy of Science. New York: Appleton-Century-Crofts, 235–252).

Duhem, P. (1962). The Aim and Structure of Physical Theory. New York: Atheneum.

Duhem, P. (1996). Essays in the History and Philosophy of Science. Indianapolis, In: Hackett.

Dunbar, R. (1995). The Trouble with Science. London: Faber & Faber.

Erwin, E. (1992). Current philosophical issues in the scientific evaluation of behavior therapy theory and outcome. Behavior Therapy, 23, 151–171.

Feigl, H. (1953). The scientific outlook: Naturalism and humanism. In: Feigl, H. and Brodbeck M. (eds), Readings in the Philosophy of Science. New York: Appleton-Century-Crofts, 8–18.

Feyerabend, P.K. (1972). Against Method: Outline of an anarchistic theory of knowledge. London: New Left Books.

Feyerabend, P.K. (1978). Science in a Free Society. London: New Left Books.

Fodor, J.A. (1987). Psychosemantics: The problem of meaning in the philosophy of mind. Cambridge, Ma: MIT Press.

Fuller, S. (1996). Social epistemology and psychology. In: O'Donohue, W. and Kitchener, R.F. (eds), The philosophy of psychology. London: Sage, 33–49.

Furnham, A. (1987). Lay Theories: Everyday understanding of problems in the social sciences. Oxford: Pergamon.

Gadamer, H.G. (1975). Truth and Method. New York: Seabury.

Gale, G. (1979). Theory of Science. Toronto: McGraw-Hill.

Geer, J.H. and O'Donohue, W.T. (1989). Introduction and overview. In: Geer, J.H. and O'Donohue, W.T. (eds), Theories of Human Sexuality. New York: Plenum, 1–19.

Gelso, C.J. (1991). Galileo, Aristotle, and science in counseling psychology: To theorize or not to theorize. Journal of Counseling Psychology, 38, 211–213.

Gorman, M.E. (1996). Psychology of science. In: O'Donohue, W.T. and Kitchener, R.F. (eds), The Philosophy of Psychology. London: Sag, 50–65.

Groenewold, H.J. (1961). The model in physics. In: Freudenthal, H. (ed.), The Concept and the Role of the Model in Mathematics and Natural and Social Sciences. New York: Gordon and Breach, 98–103.

Haught, J.F. (1995). Science and Religion: From conflict to conversation. New York: Paulist.

Hempel, C. (1953). On the nature of mathematical truth. In: Feigl, H. and Brodbeck M. (eds), Readings in the Philosophy of Science. New York: Appleton-Century-Crofts, 148–162.

Hempel, C. and Oppenheim, P. (1953). The logic of explanation. In: Feigl, H. and Brodbeck M. (eds), Readings in the Philosophy of Science. New York: Appleton-Century-Crofts, 319–352.

Holmes, J. and Lindley, R. (1989). The Values of Psychotherapy. Oxford: Oxford University Press.

Honer, S.M. and Hunt, T.C. (1987). Invitation to Philosophy: Issues and options, 5th edn. Belmont, Ca: Wadsworth.

Jevons, W.S. (1924). The Principles of Science. London: Macmillan.

Kantor, J.R. (1945). Psychology and Logic. Vol. I. Bloomington, IN: Principia.

Lakatos, I. (1976). Falsification and the methodology of research programs. In: Harding, S.G. (ed.), Can Theories be Refuted? Dordrecht: Reigel, 190–221.

Lakatos, I. (1978). The Methodology of Scientific Research Programs. Cambridge: Cambridge University Press.

Latour, B. (1987). Science in Action. Cambridge, Ma: Harvard University Press.

Leahey, T.H. (1991). A History of Modern Psychology. Englewood Cliffs, NJ: Prentice-Hall.

Lerum, K. (1998). Twelve-step feminism makes sex workers sick: How the state and the recovery movement turn radical women into 'useless citizens'. Sexuality and Culture, 2, 7–36.

MacCorquodale, K. and Meehl, P.E. (1948). On a distinction between hypothetical constructs and intervening variables. Psychological Review, 55, 95–107.

Mach, E. (1960). The Science of Mathematics: A critical and historical account of its development, 6th edn. LaSalle, Il: Open Court (original work published 1893).

Mahoney, M. (1989). Participatory epistemology and psychology of science. In: Ghoulson, B., Radish Jr, W., Neimeyer, R. and Houts, A. (eds), Psychology of Science: Contributions to metascience. New York: Cambridge University Press, 213–242.

Mahrer, A.R. (1985). Psychotherapeutic Change: An alternative approach to meaning and measurement. New York: Norton.

Mahrer, A.R. (1988). Discovery-oriented psychotherapy research: Rationale, aims, and methods. American Psychologist, 43, 694–702.

Mahrer, A.R. (1989). Experiencing: A humanistic theory of psychology and psychiatry. Ottawa: University of Ottawa Press.

Mahrer, A.R. (1995a). An introduction to some disposable myths, how to detect them, and a short list. Psychotherapy, 32, 484–488.

Mahrer, A.R. (1995b). A solution to an illusory problem: Clients construct their world versus there really is a reality. Journal of Constructivist Psychology, 8, 327–338.

Mahrer, A.R. (1996). Discovery-oriented research on how to do psychotherapy. In Dryden, W. (ed.), Research in counselling and psychotherapy: Practical applications. London: Sage, 233–258.

Mahrer, A.R. (1996/2004). The complete guide to experiential psychotherapy. Boulder, Co: Bull (original work published 1996).

Mahrer, A.R. (1997). What are the 'breakthrough problems' in the field of psychotherapy? Psychotherapy, 34, 81–85.

Mahrer, A.R. (1998). How can philosophy contribute to the advancement of psychotherapy? An introduction. Clinical Psychology: Science and Practice, 5, 229–232.

Mahrer, A.R. (1999). Embarrassing problems for the field of psychotherapy. Journal of Clinical Psychology, 55, 1147–1156.

Mahrer, A.R. (2000). Philosophy of science and the foundations of psychotherapy. American Psychologist, 55, 1115–1125.

Mahrer, A.R. (2002a). In experiential sessions, there is no therapist or client: There is a 'teacher' and a 'practitioner'. Journal of Contemporary Psychotherapy, 32, 71–82.

Mahrer, A.R. (2002b). Becoming the Person You Can Become: The complete guide to self-transformation. Boulder, Co: Bull.

Mahrer, A.R. (2003a). What are the foundational beliefs in the field of psychotherapy? Psychology: Journal of the Hellenic Psychological Society, in press.

Mahrer, A.R. (2003b). Why do Researchers do Research on Psychotherapy? Washington, DC: American Psychological Association, in press.

Mahrer, A.R. and Boulet, D.B. (1999). How to do discovery-oriented psychotherapy research. Journal of Clinical Psychology, 55, 1481–1493.

Mahrer, A.R. and Johnston, C. (2002). Promising new developments in the therapist–client relationship: A philosophy of science review and preview. Journal of Contemporary Psychotherapy, 32, 3–24.

Mill, J.S. (1862). A System of Logic: Ratiocinative and Inductive. London: Parker.

Mitroff, I. (1974). The Subjective Side of Science. Amsterdam: Elsevier.

Nagel, E. (1953). Teleological explanation and teleological systems. In: Feigl, H. and Brodbeck M. (eds), Readings in the Philosophy of Science. New York: Appleton-Century-Crofts, 537-558.

Newton-Smith, W.H. (1981). The Rationality of Science. London: Routledge & Kegan Paul.

Place, U.T. (1996). Folk psychology from the standpoint of conceptual analysis. In: O'Donohue, W. and Kitchener, R.F. (eds), The Philosophy of Psychology. London: Sage, 264–270.

Polkinghorne, D. (1992). Postmodern epistemology of practice. In Kvale, S. (ed.), Psychology and Postmodernism. London: Sage, 3–34.

Popper, K.R. (1972a). Conjectures and Refutation: The growth of scientific knowledge. New York: Harper and Row.

Popper, K.R. (1972b). Objective Knowledge. Oxford: Oxford University Press.

Popper, K.R. (1980). The Logic of Scientific Discovery. New York: Harper & Row.

Quine, W.V. (1961). Two dogmas of empiricism. In: Quine, W.V. (ed.), From a Logical Point of View. New York: Harper & Row, 20–46.

Quine, W.V. (1969). Ontological Relativity and Other Essays. New York: Columbia University Press.

Quine, W.V. (1974). The Roots of Reference. LaSalle, Il: Open Court.

Richards, P.S. and Bergin, A.E. (1997). A Spiritual Strategy for Counseling and Psychotherapy. Washington, DC: American Psychological Association.

Rorty, R. (1991). Philosophy and the Mirror of Nature. Princeton, NJ: Princeton University Press.

Rosen, H. (1996). Meaning-making narratives: Foundation for constructivist and social constructionist psychotherapies. In: Rosen, R. and Kuelwein, K. (eds), Constructing Realities: Meaning-making perspectives for psychotherapists. San Francisco, Ca: Jossey-Bass, 123–152.

Rotgers, F. (1988). Social learning theory, philosophy of science, and the identity of behavior therapy. In: Fishman, D., Rotgers, F. and Franks, C. (eds), Paradigms in Behavior Therapy: Present and promise. New York: Springer, 187–223.

Ryle, G. (1949). The Concept of Mind. London: Hutchinson.

Schlick, M. (1953). Philosophy of organic life. In: Feigl, H. and Brodbeck M. (eds), Readings in the Philosophy of Science. New York: Appleton-Century-Crofts, 523–536.

Siegel, H. (1996). Naturalism and the abandonment of normativity. In: O'Donohue, W. and Kitchener, R.F. (eds), The Philosophy of Psychology. London: Sage, 4–18.

Skinner, B.F. (1938). The Behavior of Organisms. New York: Appleton-Century-Crofts.

Speed, B. (1984). How really real is real? Family Process, 23, 511–517.

Spence, K.W. (1953). The postulates and methods of 'behaviorism'. In: Feigl, H. and Brodbeck M. (eds), Readings in the Philosophy of Science. New York: Appleton-Century-Crofts, 571–584.

Stich, S. (1983). From Folk Psychology to Cognitive Science. Cambridge, Ma: MIT Press.

Taylor, C. (1973). Peaceful coexistence in psychology. Social Research, 40, 55–82.

Toulman, S. (1953). The Philosophy of Science. London: Hutchison.

van Fraassen, B. (1980). The Scientific Image. New York: Oxford University Press.

van Fraassen, B. (1989). Laws and Symmetry. London: Oxford University Press.

Viney, W. and King, D.B. (1998). A History of Psychology: Ideas and content, 2nd edn. New York: Allyn & Bacon.

Weinsheimer, J.C. (1985). Gadamer's Hermeneutics. New Haven: Yale University Press.

Whitehead, A.N. (1929). Process and Reality: An essay in cosmology. Cambridge: Cambridge University Press.

Index

Achinstein B, 13, 46
alternative conceptual systems, 46–48
Apostel L, 27, 60
Ariew R, 17

Bacon I, 31
Barker P, 17
Bartley WW, 36
basic assumptions, 81
basic questions, 49, 56
basic truths, 25, 77–78
Bergin AE, 19
Bergmann G, 88
Boulet DB, 74
Bunge M, 36

Campbell NR, 16, 84
Carnap R, 90
cause and effect, 17
Chalmers AF, 13, 16–17, 19, 57, 80, 88
conceptual explanations, 59–63, 72–73
    rival of explanations, 67
    usefulness of, 60–63
convenient fiction, 11, 16–17, 19, 57,
    80, 88
cookbook versus explanatory science,
    26
cumulative body of knowledge, 93

definition by postulate, 16, 84
discovery-oriented research, 77
dreams, 24–25
Ducasse CJ, 69
Duhem P, 13, 17, 23, 29, 34, 36, 47, 69,
    74–76, 83–84, 86
Dunbar R, 34, 42

empirical knowledge, 75
empirical questions, 50

epistemology, 31
Erwin E, 14
euclidian geometry, 16
experiential model, 7, 21, 23, 27, 35,
    54, 61–62, 68, 81
explanation, 60–70
    bioneurophysiological levels, 70–71
    choice of, 71–72
    pictorial explanation, 69
    testing of, 69–70
external reality, 45

falsification criterion, 40, 76, 82
Feigl H, 82
Feyerabend EK, 47, 64
folk psychology, 29
Fodor JA, 29
foundational belief, 37–39
foundational truth, 49–56
Fuller S, 82, 92
Furnham A, 29

Gadamer HG, 41
Gale G, 26
Geer JH, 93
Gelso CJ, 82
Gorman ME, 83
Groenwold HJ, 64

Haught JF, 46
Hempel C, 70–71, 84, 91
high-level conceptualization, 73–74
Holmes J, 80
Honer SM, 19
human nature, 32
Hunt TC, 19
hypothesis testing, 76, 85–87
    problems in, 85–87
hypothetical construct, 18